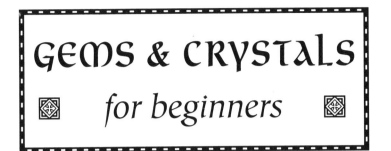

GEMS & CRYSTALS
for beginners

The publishers would like to thank R. Holt & Co. Ltd. Minerals, Stones Ltd., 98 Hatton Garden, London EC1N 8NX, Tel: 071–405 5286/0197, for providing all the stones shown in this book and Colin Taylor Productions for photographing them.

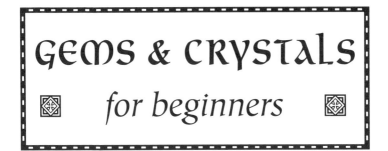

GEMS & CRYSTALS
for beginners

KRISTYNA ARCARTI

Headway · Hodder & Stoughton

With grateful thanks to Paul for his help

ΛCKNOWLEÐGEMENTS

Cataloguing and publication data is obtainable from the British Library

ISBN 0 340 60883 8

First published 1994
Impression number   10 9 8 7 6 5 4
Year   1998 1997 1996

Typeset by Wearset, Boldon, Tyne and Wear
Printed in Great Britain for Hodder & Stoughton Educational, a division of Hodder Headline Plc, 338 Euston Road, London NW1 3BH by Cambus Litho Ltd, East Kilbride

Other titles in this series

Chakras 0 340 62082 X How to work with chakras, the body's energy centres, in safety and with confidence.

Chinese Horoscopes 0 340 64804 X How to determine your own Chinese horoscope, what personality traits you are likely to have, and how your fortunes may fluctuate in years to come.

Dowsing 0 340 60882 X How to start dowsing – what to use, what to dowse, and what to expect when subtle energies are detected.

Dream Interpretation 0 340 60150 7 How to unravel the meaning behind dream images to interpret your own and other people's dreams.

Feng Shui 0 340 62079 X How to increase your good fortune and well-being by harmonising your environment with the natural energies of the earth.

Graphology 0 340 60625 8 How to make a comprehensive analysis of your own and other people's handwriting to reveal the hidden self.

I Ching 0 340 62080 3 An introduction to the ancient beauty of the *I Ching* or *Book of Changes* – its history, survival and modern day applications.

Love Signs 0 340 64805 8 The important roles played by each of the planets, focusing particularly on the position of the Moon at the time of birth.

Meditation 0 340 64835 X How to start meditating and benefiting from this ancient mental discipline immediately. Highly illustrated and full colour.

Numerology 0 340 59551 5 All the information you will need to understand the significance of numbers in your everyday life.

Palmistry 0 340 59552 3 What to look for and how to interpret what you find, using the oldest form of character reading still in use.

Runes 0 340 62081 1 How runes can be used in our technological age to increase personal awareness and stimulate individual growth.

Star Signs 0 340 59553 1 How your star sign affects everything about you. How to use this knowledge in your relationships and in everyday life.

Tarot 0 340 59550 7 Which cards to buy, where to get them and how to use them as a tool for gaining self-knowledge, while exploring present and future possibilities. Full colour.

Visualisation 0 340 65495 3 How to practise the basic techniques – to relieve stress, improve your health and increase your sense of personal well-being

CONTENTS

INTRODUCTION

The dictionary defines 'gemstone' as *a precious or semiprecious stone, especially one cut and polished* and 'crystal' as *a solid substance, such as quartz, with a regular shape in which plane faces intersect at definite angles* but these definitions say nothing about the many and varied ways in which they have been used throughout history and continue to be used today. They are so much more than attractive minerals which can be polished and made into beautiful jewellery; they have a power of their own which can help us all in our everyday lives.

The place of gemstones in history

It is said that the ancient civilisations of Atlantis and Lemuria used gemstones. Tales of the Atlanteans harnessing the power of gemstones and using it for communication over distance, and even for flight, abound. Whether you believe in the existence of Atlantis or not, it is a fact that the ancient Egyptians used gemstones for healing and attributed magical properties to many of the stones. Such beliefs continued into the Middle Ages when kings and knights wore gemstones in their breastplates as a form of protection in battle.

During our modern age, gemstones and crystals have been used in a variety of ways. Moreover, man can now 'grow' crystals for specific technological use, and lasers are just one area where man-made gemstones are used. As we move further towards the twenty-first century, the use of both natural substances and their man-made equivalents will increase.

Many people are now looking back at some of the original uses of gemstones and their fascination goes well beyond their use in jewellery, extending into the fields of health, meditation, personal guidance and individual well-being. It is with this in mind that this book has been written. Its aim is to encourage the reader to look more deeply at things which may previously have been seen in a limited context and, above all, to be sufficiently competent and confident to consider using gemstones as a means of self-help, whether this be physical, mental or emotional.

WORKING WITH GEMSTONES

During the course of this book you will learn how gemstones and minerals can help you to improve your health. You will learn how to use them for relaxation, how to stimulate your *chakras* (energy centres), and how to use gemstones to link in with your own psyche for self-improvement and personal development. We will also discuss dowsing with crystals for health reasons. On a lighter note, you will learn about the gemstones associated with the signs of the zodiac, about crystals and colour and about lucky stones.

By the end of the book, you should not only understand more about gemstones but also have the tools to understand a little more about yourself. Self-improvement is important for us all. We are all on this earth to learn and gemstones can provide a starting point on a road to increased self-awareness and improved health.

Those many people who are looking to improve their health with natural means will be glad to learn that gemstones have great potential for healing. But remember, should you be suffering with an illness, continue to follow your doctor's advice and take any medication prescribed. Continue to seek your doctor's opinion at regular intervals.

1

ϺAKING
A START

*W*hen you think about crystals and gemstones do you think of small polished stones, perhaps set in jewellery, or do you think of chunks (more properly called 'clusters') of coloured rock of varying sizes? Do you think of the uncut state, the raw natural state, or do you think of the cut stone, highly polished and sparkling? As we progress through this book, we will discuss all sorts of different types of crystals and gemstones, look at the many ways in which you can use them and explore their potential as aids in our development.

There are various reasons why people start to collect or buy crystals and gemstones. For some, it may merely be an investment for the future; for others, it may be that they like the look of the stone but have no idea of using it for anything other than a paperweight; for others, however, crystals and gemstones hold a key to the door of learning.

When you decide to start to collect crystals or to add to your existing collection, it is important to think of the reasons behind your decision. Do you want to contact your higher self? Do you want to use a stone for healing, either for yourself or someone else? Are you interested in the colour and the texture of the stones? Are you collecting stones said to match your zodiac sign? Are you interested in dowsing? Do you wish to use a crystal in a pendulum? Are you trying to rid your aura of negativities? Any or all of these might be reasons for you to purchase crystals and gemstones. Whatever the reason, it is important to learn about each crystal or gemstone so that you can use it to its full potential.

Choosing your crystal or gemstone

I have been in a shop selling crystals and gemstones and felt compelled, for a reason I cannot explain, to buy a certain stone. When this happens I always buy the stone, even if I cannot explain my choice. I know that the reason for my choice will eventually become apparent. I keep the stone in a safe place ready for its use in the future. Often I have bought a stone which has come into its own months after purchase. I have also heard it said that you should pick up a lot of crystals at the same time and whichever stone seems to 'stick' to your fingers that is the one for you.

However, when you decide to buy a stone, look at it carefully, even if it is begging you to buy it. Chipped or broken stones may have reduced energies and as such be unable to help in specific healing situations. Each stone has its own energy field, or 'piezoelectricity'. This means that there are vibrations in and around each stone. This is what gives the stones power – energy is the source of power. Anything which lessens the energy (such as a chip), reduces the efficacy of the stone, in the same way as the loss of a limb in human beings may lead to reduced abilities.

Be sure to handle the stone or crystal you intend to buy. Some people who are sensitive to energy vibrations may feel a tingling sensation with some stones whereas they feel nothing with others. Professional crystal therapists argue that to feel a tingling sensation in a crystal is a sign of negativity and that the stone should, therefore, not be purchased, as it is not meant to be used. The thing to remember is that you have to feel right with the stone, and in order to fully connect with the stone, you may find it useful to mentally ask the stone if it is right for you, or the person for whom it is intended, and see whether you get any impression one way or the other.

It is important to remember that each crystal and gemstone is unique and one may not feel the same as another. People working in shops selling crystals and gemstones are used to their customers spending time choosing the correct stones and will expect you to look at and handle many stones before you single one out. Pick up each stone in turn. If you feel happy with one, put it to one side but make sure you touch others before making a firm decision. Try the stones in both hands, not just the hand you normally use. Move them around in your hands, look at them from every angle, and buy the stone you feel happiest with.

We shall now look briefly at crystals and gemstones separately.

Choosing a crystal

If you are thinking of purchasing only crystals, remember that they are forms of quartz, naturally formed over centuries and usually imported, so they could be expensive. Quartz crystals come in many colours and with a variety of names. Pure quartz crystal is clear-coloured but amethyst is also a quartz, as are stones, such as rose quartz, milky quartz and smoky quartz. Quartz is very common. It is a powerful mineral, which has a strong link with the human race and with consciousness in particular. Crystals can come in clusters or in clear points, one end pointed and the other end not. Pure quartz crystals have six faces, but imperfections may slightly alter the structure.

The price of crystals varies enormously, depending on their quality and size. The factor which should guide you in purchase is the clarity of the stone, not the size or shape, or even the price. When you find a crystal, look carefully into its centre and satisfy yourself that there are as few imperfections as possible. If you are considering using the crystal for healing, think about the shape a little more. Some people who are using crystals for healing prefer one end to be either pointed or rounded. If you are thinking of using the crystal to enhance dreams, the shape may not be so important. If you are looking for a crystal to charge other stones or to create energy within a room, you may need to think about a larger cluster, as a larger crystal will have a larger energy field around it. Rose quartz may be the crystal to use for this sort of work. An uncut crystal is always more powerful than one which has been cut.

Choosing your gemstone

As with crystals, gemstones come in a variety of shapes, sizes and prices. Some gemstones are more difficult to excavate or to locate in the first place and so may be expensive. Lapis lazuli can be very expensive for a very small piece, for example. Whilst price may not necessarily be the main factor in your choice, make sure that you are happy with what you are getting. Again, as with crystals, look to see if the stone is chipped, imperfect or impaired in any way before making a final decision to buy. Many mineral wholesalers and gift shops know very little about the actual capabilities of gemstones, so you may be lucky and get them cheap!

Choosing a supplier

There are a number of specialist mineral agents who deal with crystals and gemstones. Many advertise in national papers as well as magazines dealing with New Age issues. In some cases, these agents offer a postal service only. It is then up to you to decide whether you feel happy about buying something you haven't seen. Personally, I always prefer to go to a shop selling crystals and gemstones and look around. There may be several in your area and I would advise you look at all the possible suppliers to ascertain the quality, as well as the price, before embarking on a definite shopping expedition.

Some stones, such as smoky quartz and citrine, can be man-made. The colours of man-made stones will not be true, and it is important to talk to the supplier, and, if possible, find out the country of origin of the stone, so you know that it is what it claims to be. Once you become used to handling stones, you will start to develop a feel for the genuine article, in the same way as someone who develops a passion for antiques learns to spot a fake.

Cleansing your stone

Now you have your crystal or gemstone, you should be aware that many people, just like you, have handled it, and it should be cleansed of any negativities it may have picked up from human contact or the environment in which it was kept. You also need to clean it in the generally accepted sense. Some maintain that the stone will have within it the memory of having been plucked from the earth and the pain associated with that excavation. Others, who are not sensitive to such matters, may disagree, but whatever you think, it is necessary to cleanse, charge and programme your new acquisition. By-passing this necessary stage can prevent the crystal or gemstone acting for you in the way in which you intend. It can also lead to headaches if you use a crystal or gemstone which is not properly cleansed of its negativities. It is important to note that the beginner may find him- or herself subject to headaches if in close contact with large crystal clusters, as the power from these is very strong. Therefore, if you are intending to use a large crystal cluster, make sure it is never kept in the bedroom, as it could cause you problems. The process of cleansing your stone is not difficult and will help you to bond with it.

CLEANSING WITH WATER

There are several ways to cleanse crystals and gemstones. One is water purification – that is to hold them under clear, running water, preferably in a natural setting. I always take my crystals to a nearby stream and cleanse them there. Other people who are unable to do this may prefer to use mineral water (not tap water) or sea water. One thing to remember about mineral water is that it may be irradiated, in which case, don't use it.

It is important to focus your thoughts on clearing the stone of its impurities. Some people always say the same few words, others say nothing but focus their attention on purity and a white or gold light. Do whatever you feel comfortable with.

If you are using bottled water, it is probably best to leave the stone in the water overnight. As the water is not running water, it is necessary for extra time to be spent if using this method. Some people like to leave their stone in the water in direct sunlight, while others who may have a connection with the moon, prefer to leave the stone in the water in the moonlight. It is said that the sun will help to energise, whilst the moon will cleanse. Generally I consider that the best time for cleansing a crystal with moonlight is during the waning of the moon, i.e. after it is into its last quarter. Others suggest the best time is during the first quarter when the moon is waxing. Again, trial and error will prove what is right for you.

CLEANSING WITH EARTH

If you feel happier using this method, you can bury your crystal overnight in the garden; should you have no garden or earth in which to bury your stone, you can use salt, preferably sea or rock salt. Again, it is necessary to focus your attention on the reasons for cleansing the stone as you bury it. Using this method may take more time and some authorities claim it is necessary to leave the stone covered in earth, or salt, for several days. Three days seems to be a generally agreed length of time. If you are using salt, make sure that you discard it once you have used it for cleansing, as it soaks up negativities which may then be transferred to a future stone. If you are burying the crystal outside, try to use an area of garden which is not cultivated and has not been polluted with pesticides or treated with fertilisers.

CLEANSING WITH AIR

You may like to try to cleanse your stone with air. There are several ways of doing this. If you feel you can offer the stone meditational breathing, you may sit with it, focusing your attention on the stone, and consciously breathe white light on the stone.

CLEANSING WITH FIRE

Using a candle or natural flame, sit in meditation with your stone and visualise the flame from the candle or fire cleansing the stone of its impurities. When you have done this, swiftly pass the stone through the flame, taking care not to burn yourself or harm the crystal in any way. This process can lead to a sooty deposit around the outside of your stone. Gently wash this off in running water and the stone will be cleansed.

How often to cleanse

Crystals which are used often or carried around regularly will need regular cleansing, and some people suggest that these crystals should be cleansed once a week.

It is important to realise that crystals soak up the atmosphere in which they are kept. If they are kept in a room where stress or tension levels run high on a regular basis, the stones will absorb this negativity and possibly need more frequent cleansing. Likewise, if a major argument occurs in a room where the crystals or gemstones are kept, it is vital that they be cleansed immediately the tensions lift, especially if you yourself have been involved in the difficulties. If you are using stones for healing, always cleanse them after a healing session as they pick up negativities from the patient.

How long to cleanse

It is worth noting that dark crystals take more cleansing than others because the energies they hold go deep. As a result, you should take more time cleansing dark stones, such as obsidian. It is also necessary to cleanse diamonds for a long time. They are a very hard stone and therefore need a long cleansing period. Man-made stones also need longer cleansing times, and zircon in particular falls into this category.

Charging your stone

Having cleansed and cleaned your crystal or gemstone, it is now necessary to charge it with the positive energies it will need to work effectively for you.

Again, there are several ways of doing this. Some people like to leave their stone in the moonlight or sunlight (either outside or in the house) for a few days, others prefer to wait for thunderstorms or very hot or very cold spells. Some people place their cleansed crystal with a programmer or generator crystal (usually a large crystal or amethyst cluster which will send out its own energies), others place their crystals and gemstones within a pyramid. The programmer crystal I have is huge and is a chunk of quartz weighing three and a half pounds and has over 80 separate crystal points, some large and some very small. It looks like a plain with a mountain rising·from its middle and is a truly beautiful object, irrespective of its energies and abilities.

An amethyst programmer crystal

The easiest way to charge your new acquisition is to sit with it in quiet and solitude and focus your attention on it in detail. If you are happy meditating, go into a brief meditation with the stone and envisage a white light enveloping both you and your stone.

Alternatively, imagine yourself going through a door within the crystal and becoming one with the stone. Imagine yourself feeling the structure of the stone and its surfaces. This process is generally best held for at least five minutes.

Some people who are unaccustomed to meditation feel quite happy charging their stones by holding them close to their hearts and picturing a calm scene – a woodland or something similar. Focusing the attention on the reason for the purchase of the gemstone or crystal will also charge the stone effectively.

PROGRAMMING YOUR STONE

Once the stone is clean, cleansed and charged it is necessary to programme the crystal or gemstone for the work it is expected to undertake. This is probably the most vital part of the process and you must be sure of the work you intend for that stone. Healing crystals must be programmed to work within a healing framework. If you are using your stone for meditational purposes, again it must be programmed to work this way. If, however, you wish to use your stone for no specific task, keep the stone in a bag or pouch, wrapped in a natural fabric, until you decide what use you intend for the stone. Some authorities suggest that you should carry the stone around with you for a month so that you bond with the crystal, should you not be programming it. Again it is up to you to do what you feel is right for you and the stone in question.

Programming the crystal involves finding a quiet place and a few minutes to relax. Place the stone between your eyebrows in the place known as the 'third eye' at the 'brow chakra', and concentrate on linking with the crystal, all the time thinking of the work you intend the stone to do for you.

CRYSTAL PLACED
ON BROW CHAKRA

It is important, as part of the programming, to dedicate the use of the crystal or gemstone for good only, which is an irreversible programme. If you even attempt to programme for evil, the stone will not accept your negative energies. If you decide to change the use of your stone, you will need to reprogramme it.

Keeping your stone

Having cleansed, cleaned, charged and programmed your stone, you must now decide upon a place to keep it.

Ideally, you should keep the stone near direct sunlight. Tradition suggests that those people who intend to use their stone for meditational or inspirational purposes should be sure to keep their stone in moonlight for several days before using it. Whatever you do, make sure that your stone sees natural light. A product of nature and of the earth, it needs natural light as much as you do, and to deprive it of this need permanently would be wrong.

If you have a large piece of crystal which you use for generating or programming, keep your new acquisition near to this. I keep my huge piece of crystal in the centre of all my other stones. This keeps them all charged and ready for use.

As with other tools of self-enlightenment, treat your crystals and gemstones with respect. Don't let anyone play with them – they are not toys. If you feel happy talking to them, by all means do so. I admit to talking to both my crystals and my plants! Show them love and consideration and they will respond.

Special types of stone

Control crystals

Control crystals are sometimes also called 'generator crystals' and should ideally be single-terminated quartz – that is one which comes to one single point. It may take a long time before the right quartz makes itself known to you. You often find that the more involved you become in crystal healing, the sooner you will find your generator crystal.

These quartz crystals can re-energise other crystals, as well as food and water. They can help to cleanse rooms of negativities as well as helping physical cleansing by being held in the hand and using a spiral movement covering the body from top to bottom and then back up again.

Jewellery

It is just as important to cleanse jewellery as it is to cleanse your newly-acquired crystals and gemstones. Jewellery, especially rings, are with you almost all the time. They pick up negativities and need cleansing regularly, in the same way as stones which stay inside your home.

The joints of the body can store negativities, which may account for the large number of people with arthritis and other joint problems, so rings, especially those with dark stones, need cleansing very often. Failure to do this can lead to rheumatic problems in the wearer. Cleansing jewellery by moonlight is probably the most effective method.

Metal is said by many authorities to inhibit healing energies, so if you are intending to buy a stone and wear it for healing purposes, or to use a stone in dowsing or as a pendulum, make sure that it has a non-metallic clasp (if worn as a necklace). If possible it should have no contact with metal at all. The best way of wearing a stone is around the neck on a thong. It is also worth noting that spherical shapes are better for healing than rough or tumbled stones.

Crystal energy rods

These rods, often quite simple structures, have been used throughout history to help tap into energy fields. They should not be confused with 'magic wands', although they do also appear in fairy tales.

Copper is the most conductive of the crystaline forms, as copper channels all forms of energy. This explains why copper bracelets are so very useful for rheumatic conditions. Crystal will help collect and amplify this 'anatonic energy' (also sometimes called 'primal energy').

Copper rods need to be capped at the end you intend to hold, as this allows interchange between the rod and the bio-plasmic energy of the body. Standard copper pipe is often used and 12 inches is the usual length.

Place the crystal at one end, avoiding the use of glue and having ensured you have pre-programmed your crystal to work with the rod. The crystal used *must* be clear quartz. Keep the copper pipe free from obstructions to allow the energy to spiral down the pipe.

Using the rod can help clear rooms of negative energies. Other gemstones can also interact with the rod, especially amethyst, but must be placed at the 'cap' end. It is important to leave the copper surface showing at the quartz end a little in order to draw in the anatonic energy.

If using a rod, make sure you feel comfortable with it and relaxed. If you intend to try using such a rod for the healing of other people, make sure they feel happy about the rod, as some people feel very uncomfortable with rods.

Absent healing stones

Using a crystal or gemstone for absent healing is a very common practice. It is worth noting that the effects of this healing can go worldwide and not just locally.

If you are thinking of buying a stone for such a purpose, it is best to think in terms of a clear, single-terminated piece of quartz crystal, with the point upright. Amethyst can be used, as can fluorite; both are carriers of a particularly strong type of energy, known as 'purple ray' energy.

Stones for absent healing must be programmed for only this function. When in use, they should be clasped with both hands and they should be stored in contact with untreated wood or earth.

We will be discussing healing in a later chapter, but for absent healing, all that is necessary is to obtain a 'signature', that is something belonging to the person for whom the healing is intended (hair, letter, photo, for example). Place your stone by this 'signature'. Ask the crystal for help for this person, not asking for a cure, but for retardation of illness or for general healing aid.

Using this process you can ask for absent healing for any number of people, in any number of places or countries, as long as each has an individual 'signature'. Once the person has recovered, or no longer needs absent healing, you can remove the 'signature', making sure you thank the crystal for its help in the process.

CRYSTAL BALLS

Nowadays, most crystal balls are not actually crystal but glass. This is because crystal is so expensive.

The purpose of a crystal ball is to act as a focus in meditational work or as an aid to developing intuition. Pictures are seen inside the globe. Some people maintain that these eminate from the subconscious, while others suggest a more mystic source. All the crystal ball does is help the person using it to focus on the work in hand, to enter into a meditative state and open themselves up to images.

Traditionally, a crystal ball should be a gift and not purchased by the person intending to use it. Mine was given to me by someone many years ago. She was not a crystal reader and had little interest in such matters, but she did have a crystal ball and gave it to me when she realised I could use it in my work.

A true crystal ball is likely to be very expensive. Again, it is necessary to cleanse, clean, charge and programme it in exactly the same way as we have discussed for crystals and gemstones, but also to polish it, preferably with a chamois leather, before leaving it in the sunlight for a few hours. After this process, nobody should touch the globe, other than you yourself. Those people coming to you wishing to receive direction from the crystal ball must not touch it. They may hold their hands above it, by all means, but never touch it. They must not look into it either.

In the next few chapters, we are going to take a much more detailed look at gemstones and crystals and discuss their use in this modern world, from both a healing and a psychological angle, but before we do, let's see how much you've remembered so far. At the end of each chapter I'll ask you a few questions, just to check on your understanding before moving on. All the answers are in the chapter you've just finished reading.

PRACTICE

- Why should you avoid buying a chipped or broken gemstone or crystal?

- Why should you not use tap water to cleanse your stone?

- Why should you cleanse your stones regularly?

- Can you use one stone for different purposes?

- Why is it important to keep healing stones away from metal?

POWER
BEHIND
THE STONES

We have already discussed some of the various uses to which crystals and gemstones can be put. We are now going to start to look a little more deeply at some of those uses.

One of the major uses for crystals is in a healing capacity, whether it be self healing, healing for others, or, as we have already discussed, absent healing.

It is very important to remember that the healing is not the same as curing. Healing is helping the body, or mind, to become stronger and consequently better. It involves looking at the person as an entity and not just at the separate symptoms. Curing is a restoration of physical health, and, in a great deal of cases, symptoms are treated rather than the individual. The restoration of physical health is the job of properly qualified doctors. Always see a doctor if you have nagging health problems – healing with crystals complements, but does not replace, medical care.

Being healthy is important to all of us. If we are to live life to its fullest potential, we need to have good health. Sometimes we fall foul of disease or illness. If you think of disease as dis-ease, a state of being ill at ease with yourself, you are half-way to understanding the bridge between the mind and the body. Crystals and gemstones can help to re-establish a broken link in that bridge and thus give the body's own healing processes a chance to work as they were intended. Often, ill-health comes about because of the stresses and strains of daily life, relationships, work, money . . . the list is endless. It is all too easy to allow outside situations to cause us problems; learning that we can do something to help ourselves overcome those problems can itself lead to an improvement in health.

ḣEALING WITḣ STONES

Over the ages, many civilisations have practised healing with crystals and gemstones. People in ancient Egypt, Tibet, India and China all used stones for healing, as did (and in some cases still do) some American Indian tribes, Australian Aboriginals and African tribes.

It is important to realise when carrying out crystal healing that we ourselves are not doing the healing. We are merely helping to alleviate blockages which allows the body to heal itself. As such, never claim you are a healer. You are merely helping the healing process. Even fully-qualified crystal therapists will never claim to be able to cure a problem. If they do, they are not sound practitioners. We will discuss visiting a therapist later on and it is vitally important to realise that the information given in this book is not sufficient to allow you to start healing others professionally. What the information will do, I hope, is to show you the various ways in which crystals and gemstones can be used and perhaps spark an interest which will stimulate you to undertake further training.

When thinking of healing, it is important to think of the physical

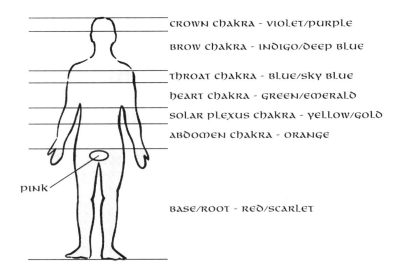

CROWN CḣAKRA - VIOLET/PURPLE

BROW CḣAKRA - INDIGO/DEEP BLUE

TḣROAT CḣAKRA - BLUE/SKY BLUE

ḣEART CḣAKRA - GREEN/EMERALD

SOLAR PLEXUS CḣAKRA - YELLOW/GOLD

ABDOMEN CḣAKRA - ORANGE

PINK

BASE/ROOT - RED/SCARLET

body, the spiritual body and the aura and chakras. We will discuss chakra centres and healing those areas specifically later, but it is vital that you appreciate from the outset that the seven chakras are the body's own energy centres, and correspond with the seven colours and the seven planets. You should also realise that your dreams may be messages from your subconscious concerning healing which the body requires.

What is required of you to start healing?

Do you have to be psychic to heal? This is a common question and the answer is that you don't, *but*, and it is a big *but*, you have to be sensitive to other people and their needs, anxieties and concerns. You also have genuinely to want to help and feel able to link with your patient with only the best intent. There are no particular hard-and-fast rules about healing with crystals but various methods can be adopted and we will discuss some of these as we progress.

One of the main requisites in being a good healer is the ability to raise the energy level of the patient. Energy rises, and it is necessary to raise energies from the bottom (the feet) to the top (the crown of head). Many healers forget this and leave their patient's energy permanently 'grounded' and then wonder why the healing energies are not working properly. It is also important to realise that you may find yourself subject to what are known as 'pranic energies' (numbness or tingling in your hands when carrying out healing). Make sure you shake your hands and wash them in cold water. Failure to do this can result in arthritic problems for you in the future.

You should bear in mind that you are a beginner and untrained. We will discuss methods of healing and how to start healing, but you must accept, and always make it clear to friends you endeavour to help through healing with crystals and gemstones, that you are not properly trained, and will not know all the answers.

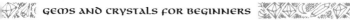

The question of diagnosis

Unless you are medically qualified, even if you become a trained crystal therapist, *never diagnose*. It is not your job to do so. You should always encourage your patient to visit their own GP or medical practitioner and make it clear that any medication prescribed *must* be taken as prescribed. People may think they know what is wrong with themselves or with others, but unless they are medically qualified or have received a medical diagnosis, they can be very wide of the mark. It is not unknown for the body to produce symptoms as a result of worry or stress which, to the untrained eye, could be taken as symptoms of a condition totally unrelated to the real problem. Remember that you are there to try to help, not create more anxieties than are already present.

Healing crystals and gemstones

We have already mentioned that a stone used for healing must be kept for that purpose alone and it is worthwhile repeating that here before we continue.

The stone or stones used for healing are special and must be kept clean and cared for. Consider keeping them wrapped in a natural fabric or in paper. However, don't forget they will still need to see regular sunlight to function properly. It is not necessary to choose only one stone for a specific problem. Remember to think of all the possible stones which could help.

If you are intending to use a personal healing stone, remember that it can be kept round your neck on a thong, but remember *no metal*. Some therapists will disagree with this but I feel confident that it is better to avoid metal wherever possible in connection with crystals and gemstones.

The other point to remember is that you must cleanse your stones regularly so they don't become blocked with negativities accumulated from people's ill-health. It is best to cleanse and clean every time you heal with a stone.

SELECTING A ROOM FOR HEALING

Make sure you use an appropriate room for healing. Those people who are skilled in the use of pendulums, or who have made themselves a pendulum from a crystal intending to use it for healing (see page 29), may like to use it to search for the most appropriate room for healing by dowsing over a sketch plan of the house. Suggest to the crystal that it looks for specific positive and negative energies in that room.

It is important that you look at the room from the outsider's viewpoint. The colours of the room are very important – they must blend and soothe. Many healing rooms are blue, as blue light in a healing room helps the client open up and discuss problems. Green is also a good colour for aiding the flow of healing energy. Any patterns in wallpaper must be flowing and wavy, rather than straight or pointed. As the ceiling area relates to the crown chakra (the top of the head), it should preferably be white, tinted with either blue or pink.

Make sure that the floor is clean and uncluttered. A dark flooring always creates a good atmosphere; patterned carpets can cause problems. Curtains should be thick enough to shut out the light, and blinds are often good for this purpose.

Lighting should be soft but it shouldn't be too dark. Spotlights, if reflecting into corners, are acceptable, but make sure the lighting is soft. Never have a light facing the door, as the person entering will see the light before anything else.

Chairs should be comfortable and not too low for people with mobility problems. People often bring friends along for moral support, so have extra chairs available, but make sure any friends sit out of the way in a corner, if possible.

The crystals you are intending to use should be kept together and be easily visible, on a trolley or table, and near to the person requiring therapy.

If you have access to a couch, use it by all means. Some people use beds, and if you are intending to do this, make sure the mattress is soft, made of natural fibres and, again, think about the colour.

You will need water, both for you and the patient. You may also need a bowl to wash your hands and a towel to dry them.

Think about a blanket for the patient. Offer it, don't force it on the person.

CREATING THE RIGHT ATMOSPHERE

Always allow the person to talk about his or her problems. Make sure you listen. Don't ask what the problem is, just listen. Make them feel wanted and make it clear that you are interested in what they are saying. People often like to be touched or greeted warmly when they come for healing. If, and only if, you are sure the person will not recoil from it, give them a hug and create some warmth and contact. Try to use first names and indulge in a little small talk to help them unwind. The chances are they will be very nervous (you may be nervous yourself) and a little chat about themselves leading on to a few words about crystals will help you both to relax.

Just say a few words about the stones and what you are going to try to do. Even if you possess lots of technical information about crystals and their properties and uses, don't bore the person with this information. Using complicated words can create barriers and we need to break down barriers, not create them. Background music can also be helpful. You should make sure you have eye contact with the person, as it helps to forge a link.

If you are intending to use different stones for the healing session, show these stones to the person. Try to sit slightly to one side of them and ask them to sit without crossing their legs or arms. Never turn your back on them, even when you are going to get your tray of stones. If you think a particular stone is appropriate for the healing, show it to the person.

If you and the person coming for therapy feel happy with crystal meditation, this is a good way of bringing about strong healing. It is important, however, that you talk this through first.

After the healing session

After a healing session, suggest the person stretches out. The healing energies will stay with them after the session itself has finished and it is important to warn them about this and explain that if they feel very tired later on, they must sit or lie down, and relax, because this is a signal that the healing is repeating itself. It is important that they understand this process. If the person has any questions, get them to ask them before they leave, before the link is broken.

Very rarely, a person will feel worse after a session. Sometimes the person accompanying them and not taking part in the healing itself may also feel rather unwell. Explain that there is still negative energy to be removed, and supply a healing crystal (such as tourmaline) or a gem elixir (discussed later on) to help. Rest should be recommended.

Natural signs of problems

You may be able to take one look at a person and have a rough idea what the problem is, especially if it relates to mobility. However, as we have already said, try not to diagnose, even mentally to yourself.

Make sure you also look for what are called 'hidden emotions'. People who are tense, nervous, avoid physical contact, sit with crossed arms or legs, have a tight smile on their lips or fidget are usually people with emotional or nervous problems. Try to get such people to talk more freely than just giving 'Yes/No' answers. Don't ask too many questions, but get them to start thinking about the crystals in a gentle, unforced way. Ask them to handle a few stones. If they feel warmth in their hands at this stage, it is an indication of healing, so saying something such as 'When you find the warmth coming, you will start to feel more relaxed and at ease' will help the relaxation process and aid in the healing.

People who are angry are difficult to work with because they often have low self-esteem. Angry people tend to give short, sharp answers and appear to bite back rather than reply naturally. They also avoid eye contact. Pyrite is very effective for such people, as we will discuss later on. People who are hyperactive can be helped with crystals, and in particular smoky quartz and haematite.

People who show such signs of negativity can have an effect on you personally, and it is important that you try not to allow this to happen, as the healing process can be impaired by your own negativities joining forces with theirs.

You may occasionally come across someone who has dependency problems on drugs or alcohol, or someone who is seriously ill. These people should be directed towards a professional crystal therapist, as the work required to help them is intense. It would also be prudent to suggest they might like other professional help and/or guidance. They must, however, seek this help of their own volition.

Dealing with a crystal rod

Once you have made sure the person feels happy with your using a crystal rod, ask them to stand with their legs slightly apart and, if possible, their arms out to the sides. If this is not possible, ask them to lie down in a similar position to the one they would have assumed, had they been standing.

Taking the rod from the left-hand side at floor level, wind it gently around the side of the person (it should not necessarily touch them) and stop at the crown. Visualise a blue colour around the person and concentrate on asking for healing energies for them. After a moment or so, gently take the rod down the other side, stopping again at ground level. Try if you can to make sure your free hand is pointing towards the ground.

If you are aware of a particular area causing concern, making sure you have one hand pointed to the earth, pass over the area with the rod, and again, envisage blue or white light.

If you are already engaged in healing of some description and are sensitive to healing energies, pass your hands over the body to scan for areas which need healing and use the rod to work on the problem, putting your other hand on the other side of the body to increase the flow of energy. You may even feel pain in your own body in the area requiring healing, but if this doesn't happen to you, don't worry. Similarly, you may be able to see auras around people. If you can, use this extra information to aid in the healing process.

All this will take several minutes. When, you feel you have done all you can at that session, take the rod from the right side of the body over the top of the crown, pausing as before to envisage the blue light, and down the other side, ending at the feet. Make sure you then take the rod back up the body and end at the crown area. It is important to circle the person a maximum of three times only.

After the healing session, if your own arms feel heavy when you raise them, take the rod and shake it behind you, making sure that the free hand is always pointing towards the ground.

Chakra healing

CROWN chakra

BROW chakra

Throat chakra

heart chakra

solar plexus chakra

abdomen chakra

base/root chakra

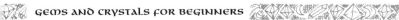

Chakras are the source of physical, emotional, mental and spiritual energy, and using crystals with the chakras can have a great healing effect. All chakras relate to colours and also to planets.

Chakras can become easily blocked – by stresses and strains, and emotional and physical problems – and it is important to check for such blockages when carrying out healing. Crystal healing removes these blockages, allowing the body's vital energy to flow freely.

Each chakra, while separate, does link with the others. As with a pair of scales where one side balances the other, one chakra should be balanced with another and I have given these, so you know which ones balance with each other. Blockages in these areas are caused by negative energies. Each chakra centre vibrates at a different rate. We will now look at each chakra centre in turn, starting at the bottom and working up. You may wish to refer to the illustration identifying the areas (see page 23) as we go through.

It is said that it is best, when working with crystals and the chakra centres to make sure that the person is facing the magnetic north. As not everyone will be aware which way is north, unless they have a compass, this can prove difficult.

If you are unsure if a chakra centre is balanced after working with it, leave an appropriate stone on it (carnelian is excellent in this respect) and continue with the healing. If at any time you are in doubt as to which stone to use for chakra clearing, again carnelian is the best bet, as it directs energy to the appropriate area.

1st Chakra ('base chakra' or 'root chakra')

Located at the base of the spine, near to the reproductive organs, this chakra sits on the coccyx. The colour of this chakra is red, its planet is Mars and it is said to relate to the earth (rather than fire, as would be assumed by the Mars connection). Its stones are garnet, ruby and red coral. Haematite and jasper, with their earthy colours, are also sometimes used, whilst some therapists consider smoky quartz is a good crystal to use when trying to clear a blockage in this chakra.

This chakra relates to sexual activity and emotions, and is also connected with the sense of smell, as it links to our animal instincts. Sometimes it is called the 'survival chakra', because it is linked to basic instincts to survive. Associated with the adrenal glands, which are situated above the kidneys, the base chakra affects the kidney and bladder (all connected with elimination of waste and toxins from the system), spine and skeletal bones, and is affected by fear, anger and sexual drive. Often a blockage in this chakra will manifest itself in back problems. A well-balanced base chakra will bring direction and contentment.

This chakra should be balanced with the crown chakra.

Clearing a blockage in the area requires the visualisation of white light entering the body at this point, with the crystal either directed towards the area or placed upon it.

2ND Chakra ('spleen chakra' or 'sacral chakra')

Located in the lower abdomen, just below the navel, the colour of this chakra is orange, its planet is the Sun, and it relates to water and the feminine side of each of us. Its stones are carnelian, orange jasper and orange coral. Orange calcite is another good stone to use when trying to clear a blockage in this chakra.

This chakra relates to digestive problems, the release of adrenalin into the system and the sense of taste. It is associated with the ovaries and testes, as it affects the function of the reproductive system, also the lower back, legs and feet. Often said to be a chakra covering happiness, freedom and openness, this chakra makes us sensitive to the needs of other people. As such, those people actively working with and trying to help others should regularly clear this chakra centre.

Men suffering problems with their prostate gland should have crystal healing on this chakra as well as the base chakra.

Problems in this area can manifest themselves in loss of self-esteem and lack of motivation. This chakra balances with the throat chakra.

Clearing the 2nd chakra involves circling the area in a clockwise direction with the crystal pointed downwards slightly. Visualisation of a white light coming from the stone to this point is important.

3rd Chakra ('solar plexus chakra' or 'hara chakra')

Located at the level of the navel in the middle of the abdomen, the colour of this chakra is yellow, its planet is Mercury, and its stones topaz, citrine and amber. Other stones which work well to clear blockages in this area are rutilated quartz, tiger's-eye and malachite. It links with the element of fire.

This chakra is closely connected to outside and external stimulii. It affects the pancreas, stomach, intestines, liver and spleen and balances with the heart chakra.

Deep emotional blockages occur frequently in this area and people with blockages here often have emotional problems and lack motivation, self-esteem and energy. As Mercury is connected with communication, people with blockages in this area are often those who need to communicate as part of their life – writers especially. Blockages in this chakra can occur through repression of anger and/ or subordination, and manifest themselves in kidney or liver problems. Increasing the level of activity of the person concerned can help to clear blockages in this chakra. Often problems with this chakra need time and patience to clear.

Clearing this chakra with crystals uses the same process as that employed in clearing the base chakra.

4th Chakra ('heart chakra')

Located in the centre of the chest and connected to the thymus gland, the colour of this chakra is predominantly green, although rose is occasionally mentioned, its planet is Venus (connected with love) and its stones emerald, green tourmaline, green calcite, aventurine, chrysoberyl and crysoprase. As rose also features in this chakra, rose quartz, rhodochrosite and pink tourmaline are also connected. This chakra links with the element of air and is connected to the breathing in of air and the ability of the lungs to nourish the body with oxygen.

The thymus gland is connected to the immune system and problems in this area can lead to a lowering of immunity from infection. This chakra interacts with the adrenal glands, affecting blood, circulation, lower lungs and breasts.

This chakra is the centre of love and emotions and blockages in this area manifest themselves in a lack of love, of self and of others. It is very much affected by self-cognition, awareness and expression of love, and the imposition of views of others. It is very hard to learn to love everyone and everything unconditionally, and therefore most of us, either permanently or occasionally, will suffer from a blockage in this chakra. Someone who is often angry or judgemental may well be subject to a blockage in this area. A well-balanced heart chakra gives compassion and understanding.

To clear a blockage in this chakra, it is best to hold the crystal a few inches away from the body and, again, visualise a white light coming from the stone directly to the point concerned.

5th Chakra ('throat chakra' or 'thyroid chakra')

This chakra is located in the throat area just below the vocal chords and is connected to sound. Its colour is blue, its planet the Moon, its stones aquamarine, turquoise, blue topaz and blue lace agate and it connects with space. Some therapists suggest lapis lazuli should be used for this area but I would disagree. Lapis is much better used on the 6th chakra.

Associated with the thyroid gland, it affects the pharynx, larynx, gums, tongue, upper lungs, shoulders, arms and hands, as well as the lymphatic system.

Blockages often manifest themselves in lung problems, catarrh and sometimes eye problems. The correct functioning of this chakra is affected by mental states and people with blockages in this area often find themselves unable to express themselves properly, probably as a result of their suppression by others. Stress, anxieties, hidden emotions and fears can also block this chakra. A well-balanced chakra will bring about open-mindedness, good communication, creativity and self-expression.

As this chakra is connected to sound, it is possible to work on clearing a blockage with the use of sound. Many people suggest that the use of mantras helps, while others suggest the use of music. To clear a blockage with crystals, place the stone a little way from the centre and, again, visualise white light.

6th Chakra ('brow chakra' or 'third eye chakra')

Located between the eyebrows, this chakra is connected with indigo, the planet Jupiter and the stones sapphire, lapis lazuli, sodalite, purple fluorite, azurite and amethyst.

Related to matters psychic or spiritual, this chakra is associated with the higher functions of the mind, the pituitary gland, hypothalmus, frontal lobes, one or both eyes (usually the left), the ears and the sinuses.

This chakra is the co-ordinating chakra for all others and is affected by the desire to be open-minded.

Fear is one of the signs that this chakra is blocked and when all is well in this chakra, one is less affected by worry and doubts. Headaches and vision problems also indicate a blockage.

To clear a blockage in this chakra, the crystal should be held a few inches away from the area, pointing downwards, and should be rotated gently in a clockwise direction for several minutes.

7th Chakra ('crown chakra')

Located at the top of the head, this chakra has as its colours violet, gold and white and is connected with the planet Saturn and with the stones amethyst, sugilite, diamond, gold fluorite and clear crystal quartz.

This chakra concerns spiritual desires and is associated with cerebral functions. Often people who suffer seasonal depression (SAD) have blockages in this area.

A well-balanced crown chakra brings about perfect awareness and enlightenment, whereas a blocked one creates a selfish and negative person. Connected with total oneness with the universe and with nature, many people would do well to work more with this chakra.

This chakra balances with the base chakra and when properly open will bring about creativity, happiness and a feeling of being at peace and in good health.

To clear a blockage in this chakra, point the crystal downwards towards the top of the head, turning it in clockwise circles and again visualising white light. This may take some time, and you may find your arm begins to ache. Should this happen, sit quietly with the crystal and continue the meditation for a while longer.

Working with pendulums

Dowsing with a pendulum is really easy. Most people start with a piece of quartz crystal or, alternatively, amethyst, on a thong. Watch which way the pendulum swings on questions requiring a 'Yes' or 'No' answer to which you already have the answer. This will tell you how your pendulum indicates 'Yes' and 'No'. Normally speaking, the three possible responses for the pendulum are it moving from left to right, right to left or in a circular pattern. After finding the 'Yes' response, ask for a 'No' response as well as a 'Don't know' response – again by asking questions to which you know the answers.

You can use the pendulum to answer questions on vitamin deficiencies, allergies and any health problem requiring a 'Yes' or 'No' answer, but one of the easiest ways to use the pendulum is in chakra work. Merely by watching how the pendulum swings will give you the answer to the question of blockages, using the 'Yes'/ 'No' technique already discussed.

To do this sort of work, merely hold the pendulum in one hand, and touch the various chakra points with your other hand. Asking whether the chakra is blocked or not, watch which way the pendulum swings, and you will be sure to get your answer. Working then to clear the chakra as discussed above will provide the necessary healing.

If you are interested in dowsing in general and not only for health, you might like to read *Dowsing for Beginners* by Naomi Ozaniec, another book in this series.

CRYSTAL MEDITATION

If you want to use crystals for meditational healing, but have not done so before, start with amethyst. It is a powerful stone and a good and gentle healer and is especially useful in treating nervous conditions and anxiety. Another powerful stone is quartz crystal and you may progress on to use aquamarine. However, whatever you choose, make sure that the stone or stones you use are programmed for crystal meditational healing only.

Before beginning any form of healing with crystals by meditation, make sure to ask for protection for yourself and the other person, as well as for the crystal.

Some people using crystal meditation for healing merely place a very large crystal in the room between the 'patient' and helper; others suggest a small tray of crystals is placed between patient and helper. It is equally acceptable for both parties to meditate with separate crystals.

If you are working alone to heal another person, try to link with the crystal and with them, sit facing each other, thinking of good and imagining healing energies being directed to the area causing the concern. Close your eyes and ask the other person to do likewise, gently relax into the meditation and concentrate on the white healing light being directed to the problem area.

Sessions such as this should last up to 20 minutes maximum. The main emphasis should be trying to be at peace with the crystal, and it is important after the meditation finishes to thank the crystal for its help.

Often groups get together to meditate with crystals for healing purposes. If you are about to form such a group, try to nominate someone to be in charge of the stones, care for them and cleanse them. Ideally the crystals should be placed in the middle of a circle and meditation commence after that. This creates a balanced energy.

Aura Healing

The aura is the body's own energy pattern visible outside the body. Some people are able to see auras easily with their own eyes, while others are not so fortunate. However, being unable to see the aura of people should not indicate to you that it isn't there. All it should indicate is that you are unable to see it.

The aura surrounding the hands, as shown by Kirlian photography

Working on the aura is very effective; all that is necessary is true intent to heal and help and a strong healing crystal. Again amethyst is a good crystal with which to start.

Holding the crystal in your left hand, even if you are right-handed, pass the crystal gently around the aura of the person concerned. If you are sensitive to such things, you may find yourself stopping or slowing down in a particular area. This could indicate a break in the aura at that point. Should this happen, visualise the crystal sending energies out to heal the break and continue to cover the whole of the aura. No contact with the body is necessary and this healing only need be carried out a maximum of twice weekly.

This method can also be used in cases of specific physical injury, when all that is necessary is to pass the crystal over the injured area, asking for healing energies to be released by the crystal into the aura at that point.

Dreams

Before we end this chapter, we will briefly discuss dreams. Many students of crystal therapy suggest that sleeping with a crystal or gemstone beneath the pillow will help the sleeper to remember their dreams. Often when we are ill, we have dreams which relate to our state of mind and our illness. Sometimes we remember such things but often this is not the case. The question to consider is whether it is beneficial for our conscious mind to remember and work on our dreams as an aid to regaining our mental and physical health.

Should you feel the need to recall your dreams and to try this form of self-help, a quartz crystal or amethyst beneath the pillow at night may help, but make sure you also keep a piece of paper and pencil by the bedside, so that you can record everything on waking. Sodalite is also used for dream retention.

Just before we go on to look at the major healing stones in detail, let's see how much you've remembered from this chapter.

PRACTICE

- Describe the main steps involved in healing with a crystal rod.
- What are chakras?
- How can you get answers to questions using a pendulum?
- What is a good stone to start with for crystal meditation?
- What is an aura?

STONES FOR HEALING

We are now going to take a look at 15 of the major healing stones, discussing, where applicable, traditional and modern thought on their healing properties. We will also take a look at elixir oils made from crystals and gemstones.

Before we discuss each stone in detail, it is important to mention the placebo effect, which sceptics will raise at every possible opportunity. The placebo effect asserts that a person will feel better after treatment if they expect that they will, even if the healing they are receiving is worthless. Sometimes the placebo effect has been cited as being the only reason for any noticeable improvement in health when crystal therapy is employed. When somebody says to me that crystal healing is all in the mind, I point out that many problems start in the mind and spread to the body.

My 15 top healing stones

The information I give in the following pages is based on current thought on the healing qualities of the 15 stones I most often work with. However, this does not necessarily mean that the 15 stones listed here will be the 15 stones used by all crystal therapists. Many therapists compile different lists based on the work they undertake and the results they achieve. It is therefore up to the individual to decide which of these stones to use and which to leave out.

AMAZONITE

A powerful stone, blue-green in colour and having in it a trace of copper. It is said to help with nervous problems and mental anguish, and is sometimes referred to as the 'Amazon stone'. This pale green stone is a feldspar mineral, believed by crystal therapists to have particularly good powers of repairing the body. It comes from Brazil and is said to provide strength, help soothe the nerves and give added auric healing – thus it is often used in healing the aura, providing emotional help and support in times of trouble. Those engaged in creative work will often find this gemstone of use, as it is said to help provide perspective and rid the system of negativities. I always think of Amazonite as one of the major stones for emotional and mental problems.

Amazonite was valued greatly by the Egyptians. It is not expensive, and is relatively easy to obtain.

AMETHYST

We have already mentioned this especially powerful spiritual stone. Said by some New Age followers to be less powerful than fluorite, which also carries the purple ray, amethyst is, in my opinion, an essential part of any crystal or gemstone collection, whether used for healing, self-help or meditational purposes. The amethyst belongs with the quartz family and the purple colour in the stone is due to small traces of iron.

Linking with the zodiac (see chapter 6) this stone is often used for helping to gain psychic knowledge. It gives protection to those who wear and use it and Christian crusaders often attached it to their rosaries in this belief. I personally always have a piece of polished amethyst on my person, whether in jewellery or on a pendulum, and have several pieces, of various sizes, in my collection of stones for healing purposes.

Healers of times gone by suggested that this stone could help in dream revelation, as discussed in the last chapter, and you could try this for yourself (you must be sure to use a smooth piece). Many claim that it will help with inspired dreams and give clarity of thought if put under the pillow at night, or, attached by gauze to the wrist, will relieve insomnia and bring peace and harmony. Amethyst is a stone which can help with a wide variety of problems, as it is a spiritual stone which inspires the healing of all the organs and brings about mental peace.

I always think of amethyst as a stone of love, not only of human love but of divine love. If we learn to love ourselves and to love others unconditionally, we will all experience a greater sense of well-being.

AQUAMARINE

This is another stone used in cases of nervous problems. This stone is 'of the sea', as its name reflects, and I have found it works especially well with those people who are water signs in the zodiac, or who have a strong connection with the sea or maritime affairs. This beautiful blue-green beryl can, unfortunately, be heat-treated to become bluer, so be sure when buying this gemstone that you are getting the untreated stone. Beware also of stones which look like aquamarine which are in fact spinel or glass. It is always important to buy your stones from a reputable supplier who knows and understands about gems and crystals.

I have tried taking pieces of aquamarine into exams with me and have usually found that I feel more at ease with the stone than without it. If you have an exam coming up, this is surely worth a try.

Another property of this stone is its ability to help with stomach and thyroid problems. Especially strong if used in meditation for such problems, this stone will help to cleanse the body and can also be effective in cases of migraine. However, as it is a particularly powerful meditational stone, it should only be used by those people sufficiently practised in meditation to be able to cope with working on a deeper level.

Its connection with the sea is extended to suggest that it is useful for fluid retention problems and, again, I have tried this with quite a considerable degree of success, especially for those people born under the sign of Cancer the Crab, which links with water and also the moon, the latter controlling the ebb and flow of the tides. Further information on the zodiac link with this stone appears in chapter 6.

CALCITE

This is an excellent stone to use in cases of fear and anxiety. It is often used to help those who suffer badly with stress-related problems and emotional disorders. The deep-blue calcite is used widely for deep healing, the colour blue itself being a particularly good healing colour. Calcite can also come in white, yellow, red, green, brown, black, transparent and grey.

True calcite can easily be cut with a knife, as it is a relatively soft stone, and is commonly known as 'alabaster'. Calcite is found in large quantities in Egypt and was used by the ancient Egyptians. It is also known as limestone, marble and chalk.

Calcite helps with kidney problems. Alongside snakeskin jasper, it is often used for skin problems. Calcite is another very good meditational stone, and I can definitely recommend its use in this type of work.

CARNELIAN

Another stone with a zodiac link, carnelian, with its red colour which stems from iron oxides, is said to help with blood disorders and the elimination of waste products and toxins from the body. Another powerful healer, it helps to restore any broken links between the physical body and the spiritual body and is therefore widely used in auric healing. It is also often used in chakra balancing when there is doubt as to whether the chakra is balanced or not. It is a 'thinking stone' and an excellent healer. It helps to focus the mind on any project requiring concentration.

In the past it was used to help stop nosebleeds and soften anger. It was thought by the Moslems to fulfil all desires. King Alphonso X of Spain believed it improved voice projection. Nowadays this stone is more commonly used to help those with stress-related problems to be 'grounded' and balanced. Some texts suggest that it can be used as a tonic for the blood, but I am unable to comment on this, as I have never used it for that purpose.

I have often used this stone in meditation, as its warm red colouring helps in relaxation and focuses the mind.

CITRINE

I always think of citrine with its bright yellow tones as a stone of communication. This yellow quartz is fairly rare in its pure state and may be difficult to obtain. Those outlets which seem to have lots of citrine available for sale may in fact be dealing with an artificially-produced product, as it is possible to turn amethyst yellow by heat-treatment. To tell the difference, look closely at the stone. Natural citrine will be cool and pale and seem to have a greenish tint to the yellow colouring. Artificially produced citrine will exhibit red, or even orange, shades within its depths.

Many people find at some time during their lifetime they need help to be able to communicate effectively, whether this be at work, in personal relationships or merely in a general sense. I have found that citrine helps with this. The yellow colour is a natural reviver, and the citrine will help promote a feeling of self-esteem, which in turn will aid communication.

I know of crystal therapists who use this stone to help people find their true path in life, and once again, there are times when this may be tried. There are few people who go right through life with a sense of purpose and, if you personally feel that you need some direction, you may wish to try using the citrine, particularly in meditation, as it could help re-establish the link between your conscious and subconscious minds. If you are feeling down, try holding a citrine for a while, as it will help lift your spirits.

FLUORITE

Thought by many to be the most important healing stone for the Age of Aquarius, fluorite is indeed a powerful gemstone, which was overlooked for many years, although it was a favourite with ancient civilisations – pieces of fluorite were excavated in the ruins of Pompeii. In more recent times, it has been heralded as the symbol of the growth of humanity and a strengthener of bone tissue. As such, it is often thought to be beneficial to women suffering from osteoporosis.

Blue John, mined in Derbyshire, England, is a form of fluorite, and it comes in varying colours, from deep, dark purple, to pink, green, yellow and blue, depending upon its source. As it is very easily scratched, it is seldom used in jewellery.

Fluorite is definitely a stone whose colours influence its useage but broadly speaking, it is a repairer and builder. In its purple variety, many suggest that it is as useful in healing as amethyst.

Fluorite will help bring peace and calm to a troubled mind and holding even a very small piece in the hand can bring about a sense of calm. Another stone which is particularly useful in meditation, it will help to calm even the most excitable person and promote a feeling of inner peace.

Pink fluorite will be expensive but other forms are relatively cheap.

Lapis Lazuli

Sometimes also called 'lazurite', this stone has strong Egyptian, Sumerian and Biblical links, its name stemming partly from the Arabic word for 'blue' and partly from the Latin for 'stone'.

Said to be useful for people suffering from insomnia, its dark-blue colour with specks of gold can lead to its being confused with azurite and lazulite, which are different minerals entirely.

A popular healing stone for several centuries, lapis should, in my opinion, be used with care, as it is extremely strong and powerful and can lead to problems for those who are not able to cope with its properties.

In ancient times, it was used to cure skin problems and blood disorders. In more modern times it has been used as a healer for many diseases, from eyesight problems to fevers. Lapis lazuli is another good meditational stone, which helps to strengthen the body and promotes self-assurance.

Some people seem to have a natural affinity with lapis lazuli, and if this applies to you, you will find it will help to develop any psychic abilities you may have and increase your sensitivity. It is for this reason that I recommend it be used with care. I am particularly sensitive to lapis lazuli, and even holding a small piece for a minute will produce heightened sensitivity which can, if I'm not careful, lead to headaches and other such problems. As it can help to create a stronger bond between the spiritual and physical, it is a very good healing stone and is often used in cases of depression.

Sodalite, which is another blue stone, can be made to look like lapis, as can jasper if dyed correctly, chalcedony and synthetic ultramarine. Glass or even plastic are sometimes passed off as lapis.

OBSIDIAN

Obsidian is a natural glass formed from volcanic lava, usually black, hard, shiny and strong and used by many ancient civilisations for healing. The Aztecs used it to make knives, spears and arrowheads.

Obsidian can sometimes be brown/red in colour and snowflake obsidian has white flecks.

Professional crystal therapists usually recommend that obsidian should be balanced with a lighter crystal, such as snowy quartz, when used in a healing capacity. It is not recommended for use in absent healing. Used for relieving stomach problems and clearing the mind, it helps to balance confusion when combined with snowy quartz, as it represents the material or earth aspect of activity whereas snowy quartz represents spiritual acitivity.

It is sometimes used as the basis for 'magic mirrors' which are used as a means of obtaining images, in much the same way as the crystal ball. As such, it is often considered to be a tool towards spiritual awareness. Gazing into even a small piece of obsidian can be a wonderful experience. It has a depth which is indescribable, and only personal practice will enable the reader to fully understand its powers.

PYRITE

Often termed 'fool's gold' this stone is frequently used in the making of jewellery, when it is passed off as marcasite, although true marcasite is quite different and less adaptable.

Mexican Indians used pyrite for their magic mirrors rather than obsidian. Used by professional crystal therapists extensively on any addiction problems, it allows the person to connect with the earth's energy and is said to help strengthen the will.

Modern usage seems to be mainly directed towards lung or

breathing problems, as well as digestive disorders and depression.

QUARTZ CRYSTAL

Quartz crystal is one of the three most important stones for healing, the other two being amethyst and fluorite. Said to generate and amplify electricity from the healer to the patient, quartz unblocks energy centres and helps the body to heal itself. Having achieved a state of well-being, many therapists suggest that simply holding a piece of quartz crystal each day will help to boost the immune system and stave off future illness. It should be noted, however, that mineralogists suggest that quartz neither conducts nor amplifies electricity. Quartz crystal is a valuable aid in self-healing and can be used in single point or cluster form. Many programmer or generator crystals are clusters of quartz crystal.

When referring to 'crystal', many therapists mean quartz crystal. I use the term 'quartz crystal' to refer to clear quartz. Other coloured varieties (such as rose quartz) are referred to separately.

There are many types of coloured quartz in addition to rose quartz, for example snowy quartz, smoky quartz, rutilated quartz (which can be clear or smoky), citrine, amethyst, tourmalinated quartz and aventurine.

About an eighth of the world's crust is quartz, and it has been used in buildings for thousands of years. Many ancient people mistakenly believed clear quartz to be fossilised ice. Roman ladies used to carry quartz balls around to cool their hands when the weather turned warm. American Indians used quartz for divining purposes and other ancient peoples used the stone for cauterising wounds.

The greatest use for quartz crystal is in meditation. It is excellent when used in deep meditations, as it seems to help the mind to focus. Its main usage should perhaps be to help heal the mind rather than the body, although many therapists use it when carrying out chakra healing, as it is said to dispel negativities.

ROSE QUARTZ

Rose quartz ranks alongside amethyst in my personal preference list. Its beautiful, gentle, pink shade seems to have a healing quality in its own right. It is usually found in chunks, as it does not form individual crystals.

An important stone in chakra healing, it seems to deal with the heart of the individual and with love and emotions. Holding a piece of rose quartz invariably leads to a feeling of inner peace, and those suffering from trauma would be well directed to sit with a piece of rose quartz, and perhaps enter into meditation, if this is an activity with which they feel comfortable.

A calming stone, it exposes emotional unbalances. It is said that a piece of rose quartz in a room where tensions are likely to rise will stop matters reaching boiling point. I have tried this on occasions, sometimes with success.

Useful in reducing cases of high blood-pressure, certain therapists suggest that the stone is beneficial in dealing with heart problems and as a diuretic. Others are more specific, suggesting it helps the kidney area and is a stimulant to the circulation. I cannot comment on this claim, as I have yet to try the stone in this connection, but I can say that it is a very good stone to use for emotional problems and is exceptionally effective in meditation and as a stress-reducer. I have used it in the treatment of headaches and migraines which may be stress-related.

SODALITE

Sodalite is a lovely blue stone, sometimes peppered with white calcite. It is helpful for those who suffer with anxieties and nervous problems. Said to balance the mind, it helps people who are highly strung to be a little more focused and rational. It is another stone believed to lower blood-pressure.

People who suffer with nervous trouble may well wish to wear it regularly, especially in situations which they feel may prove stressful.

Sodalite may also help promote communication and encourages forms of self-expression.

A piece of sodalite under the pillow may help you remember your dreams.

TIGER'S-EYE

Another member of the quartz family, tiger's-eye is golden yellow and brown. It is often polished to make tumble stones, eggs, beads and pyramids and makes eye-catching jewellery.

For years, I have carried a piece of tiger's-eye around in my purse. The reason for this is that it helps to counteract nervous or stress-related illnesses, increases self-confidence and benefits the digestive system. It is also said to give those who carry it clearer perception and is particularly useful in business dealings.

Popular with those people who study Chinese philosophies, this stone, with its layers of dark colouring next to bright colouring, seems to be the epitome of the Yin/Yang principle – i.e. the principle of male and female, or negative and positive, working together in harmony.

Meditating with this stone should be left until the art of meditation at a deep level has been successfully attained.

TOURMALINE

Tourmaline gets its name from the Sinhalese *turmalli*, which means 'mixed precious stone', and indeed no other gemstone has so many colourings and varieties. It can be brown, orange, green, blue, black, dark green, yellow and many other colours. One stone can have within it as many colours as you care to name.

Watermelon tourmaline has a blue/green outer layer and is pink/red inside. It is particularly good for meditation in this form, although claims that it can alter the structure of cells are probably false.

Said to benefit those suffering with nervous problems, especially if worn against or close to the skin, it is sometimes known as the 'confidence stone', as it helps dispel fear and negativities and helps those using it to face adversity. It is particularly useful in dealing with mental anguish, possibly because of its wonderful colourings.

We have now covered what in my opinion are the 15 main healing stones. As you will have gathered, certain claims for the healing properties of the stones may be over-ambitious, but I leave it up to the individual to carry out his or her own research into the stones and decide in which way to use each crystal or gemstone. Remember, doctors are the proper people to treat physical illness, crystal therapy complements, but does not replace, orthodox medicine.

Gemstone elixirs and oils

Before finishing this chapter, we will briefly look at gemstone elixirs and massage oils. Gem elixirs are usually made from water in which the relevant stone has been soaked.

They can be used as a means of drawing the healing vibrations of the crystals into the body.

Making your own elixir

It is possible to make up your own gem elixir using filtered water which has been sterilised and purified. It is best not to use bottled water as it may have been irradiated. Once you have a bottle of water put your gemstone in it and leave it *in the sun* for four hours. You should always use a stone which has been programmed for healing purposes and also perhaps programmed to work within a gem elixir. It is said that the best time to make an elixir is the two hours either side of midday. Remove the stones and pour the elixir into 10 ml bottles, filling two thirds of the bottle. Fill the other third with pure alcohol (vodka is acceptable), label and shake occasionally to prevent stagnation. The shelf-life of elixir is only three months.

It is possible to make an elixir using more than one stone, and if you are thinking of doing this, try to use a carnelian as they are excellent for gem elixirs. They seem to direct the energy to the most appropriate place for healing. If in doubt which stone to use for your elixir, carnelian (the thinking stone) is the best one to use.

If you feel you need a gem elixir quickly and have not had sufficient time to make one (say you have only had two hours rather than the four required) it is possible to speed up the process by placing the bottle or elixir in a glass on a cluster or within a crystal triangulation (three crystals in a triangular shape).

Taking the elixir

Using a gem elixir requires you to be in a calm and relaxed state. It is recommended that you take a few deep breaths and hold the bottle before actually taking the elixir, and then place three or four drops in the mouth, preferably under the tongue. Three drops of the gem elixir can be placed in a cup of tea to relieve stress and depression. It should be taken at least 30 minutes before or after a meal.

Citrine and aventurine are said to lift the energy of a person, whilst yellow and red calcite and turritella agate will lift a person's confidence and self-esteem. A note of caution – don't use gem elixirs too often, as you can cause over-stimulation by doing so. Occasional use is the best advice with such potions. If you feel ill on taking an elixir, *stop at once*.

Elixir oils

Elixir oils, similar to aromatherapy oils, are another form of treatment. The skin absorbs the oil and helps the body open up to the healing vibrations of the stone.

To make an elixir oil, use any natural oil, vegetable, nut or fruit. Cold-pressed, virgin olive oil is a good releaser of blockages. Most therapists suggest grapeseed as the best carrier because it is good for skin cleansing and helps eliminate toxins. Wheatgerm oil is another good carrier and especially good for damaged skin. Most aromatherapists will suggest sweet almond oil, as it is very easily absorbed, non-greasy and an excellent healing oil.

Place the stones directly into the oil, avoiding contamination from dirt. Charge your oil elixir under a pyramid shape or in a triangle made by three crystals. It is said that moonlight-charged elixirs can be used for emotional problems with good results and that leaving elixirs in the moonlight will also help with fluid-retention problems (again relating back to the waxing and waning of the moon and its effects on the tide). Amethyst is a good stone to use for stress and tension and rock quartz will help with back problems. An oil made of wheatgerm and aventurine is said to be good for stretch marks, if used twice daily.

Before applying the oil elixir, use the thumb and palms to warm and stimulate the skin. Use the palms of the hand to apply the oil initially and massage gently.

Do not take gem elixir oils internally. They are for massage purposes only.

We have now looked at the major stones and are ready to start looking at specific health problems and how they may be helped by using crystal therapy, but before we do, you might like to ask yourself the following questions to see how much you have remembered about this chapter.

PRACTICE

- Which stone might help you stay calm in an exam?
- Which stone is formed from volcanic lava?
- What are three of the most important stones for healing?
- What is the best time to make gem elixirs?
- How do you use elixir oils?

everyday health

*I*t is important to remember that crystal and gemstone therapy should not replace the medication or medical advice given by your doctor or physician. Crystal and gemstone therapy can help to speed healing but if your complaint continues to be troublesome, it is always best to consult your doctor. In that way, this form of healing can complement the medication and advice given to you.

Many people use the term 'alternative therapy' to describe any treatment other than the conventional medical help you would receive from your doctor, but I feel this leads one to dismiss orthodox medical help as being unnecessary, which is not the case. Whereas chiropractic, acupuncture, herbalism, homoeopathy and naturopathy might be called 'alternative therapy', gemstone and crystal therapy is much more accurately described as 'complementary therapy'. There is a place for complementary therapies alongside the more orthodox forms of healing and crystal and gemstone therapy should be seen in this light.

I firmly believe that we can help our bodies to heal themselves and that our mental approach can be of paramount importance in speeding up any healing process. It is therefore essential that trust be placed in any therapy given, whether this be at the hands of your physician or at the hands of your crystal and gemstones therapist. Indeed, healing can also come from your own hands and in this chapter we are going to discuss this further. We will not only look at which crystals may be able to help in treatment of the condition concerned but will also briefly discuss any self-help measures which should be taken into account.

Treating physical complaints

MIGRAINES

One of the commonest complaints, especially among those who are subjected to high levels of stress, is the type of headache called 'migraine' – headaches with neurological symptoms, such as numbness, distorted vision or weakness down one side of the body.

Although stress is one of the main causes of migraines, they can be related to diet and cheese, coffee, chocolate and other foods often lead to an attack. Women taking oral contraceptives may also find they become subject to migraines, and if this is the case, the doctor should be informed.

TREATMENT

Self-help measures obviously include cutting down, or even cutting out, any dietary substance which may trigger an attack, and trying to be aware of potentially stressful situations and endeavouring to deal with them calmly.

The stones most commonly used to help with migraines are jet, aventurine and rose quartz. These can be used by working on the brow chakra, as discussed earlier, or by merely holding the stone on the forehead and taking deep breaths. A few drops of elixir oil may also be massaged on to the temples and stomach to ease the problem. Auric healing may also be of use.

I have found it is best to use these treatments as early as possible before the full-blown migraine develops. After an acute migraine has developed, however, the therapies using crystals and gemstones can still help, but should be combined with rest in a darkened room.

DEPRESSION

There are few things more generally debilitating than depression. Some people suffer depression which is so bad that they are forced to seek psychiatric help. It should be clear here that we are not trying to deal with people who suffer with manic depression or a serious depressive disorder, or those who are suffering from postnatal depression. People suffering from such problems should be directed to their doctor and only when the situation begins to improve should they seek help from crystals and gemstones. Any depression which lasts more than a few weeks always needs the help of a doctor or physician.

TREATMENT

When dealing with depression, the most common crystals and gemstones are emerald, jasper, smoky quartz and occasionally zircon. Other stones such as amethyst, aquamarine (especially for nervous depression), tourmaline and fluorite can help, and I always feel it is best to offer a variety of stones to someone in this position and allow them to choose a stone with which they personally feel comfortable.

In addition to crystal and gemstone therapy, those suffering from depression would be well advised to take more exercise, as depression can often stem from bottled-up stress and emotion, which can be released through exercise which lasts in excess of 20 minutes.

It is also sometimes useful to keep a diary, talk things over with other people who are willing to listen and to learn to express pent-up emotions and anxieties. Professional crystal therapists often deal with people who are suffering from depression and are more than happy to listen to the problems being experienced. Many professional crystal therapists will use the ruby on an initial visit, putting it on the heart or base chakra centres.

Learning to relax is also very important in overcoming depression and meditation, with any of the crystals discussed in the last chapter, is likely to be of benefit. It may also help to carry around the chosen crystal or gemstone, as it will then help the healing process throughout the day.

SKIN PROBLEMS

Skin problems can cover a multitude of differing ailments, such as cold sores, hives, acne, bruising, boils and pimples, eczema, psoriasis, ulcers and even skin cancers.

We are concerned here with *minor* skin problems. Major problems must receive medical attention. Do not try to treat moles with crystals; go to your doctor. Go to your doctor if any symptoms persist.

TREATMENT

Many skin complaints, such as blisters and boils, benefit from exposure to air and simply being kept clean, and this should be the first course of action with such problems. Boils in particular can be a sign of stress, as they usually appear when a person is run down or weakened by a poor diet. Anything, therefore which can aid relaxation will be of benefit.

Oil elixirs may help with these sorts of skin complaints and should be used with gentle massage. An oil elixir made from snakeskin jasper is very good for the skin.

Cold sores are caused by the herpes simplex virus and often lie dormant in people, to appear at times of stress or fever. Taking extra B complex vitamin often helps with cold sores and using an oil or one made with wheatgerm oil may also help.

With regard to other skin problems, agate, aventurine, cat's-eye, red coral and sapphire may aid in the healing process and can either be used as oil elixirs or alone by putting the gemstone or crystal on the area in question and seeking healing in that way. Cat's-eye and red coral are said to be particularly effective in cases of eczema. Aventurine gem elixir made with water is particularly good for minor skin irritations and should preferably be made the day before, left overnight, and then used to gently bathe the affected area. Calcite and snakeskin jasper are also often used to treat general skin problems. Amethyst cluster is often used for ruptured tissue, burns, sprains and grazed skin and rose sand crystals are good for skin repair.

It should be remembered that skin problems may be a result of an allergy to a material, a food substance or something such as a new washing powder. It is best to eliminate these possibilities as a matter of course before commencing any form of crystal or gemstone therapy.

Rheumatism

Pain and stiffness in joints, which are the main symptoms of rheumatism, can strike at any age, although relatively more people over the age of 50 will suffer with this complaint. Always see your doctor if you suffer prolonged pain in your joints.

TREATMENT

One of the oldest ways to treat rheumatism is the use of copper. Many people wear copper bracelets and those stones with a trace of copper may also help.

Generally speaking, however, the most popular stones for the treatment of this complaint are lodestone, an iron oxide, or magnetite and malachite, which both contain traces of copper. Turquoise also contains copper traces, as does dioptase, chrysocolla, and azurite, and these may be tried.

Malachite made into a gemstone elixir may relieve rheumatism and a few drops can be taken in a cup of tea.

INSOMNIA

Insomnia, the inability to get to sleep or to stay asleep, is something which affects almost everyone at some time in their lives. Drinking coffee, noise, worry, anxiety and pain can all lead to an inability to get to sleep.

TREATMENT

The ability to relax certainly plays a large part in whether a person manages to get a good night's sleep, or not. If you are worried about something or in pain, you will not be relaxed, and therefore are likely to experience problems in achieving the necessary state for sleep.

Taking more exercise should always be considered if insomnia becomes a problem. Other self-help measures should include a warm milky drink at night (not coffee), a warm but well-ventilated bedroom, a comfortable bed or sleeping position, and a warm bath just before retiring. Try not to eat late at night, as your sleep-pattern will be disturbed. Those of a nervous disposition should try to avoid watching late night horror films or thrillers either on TV or video. Another good piece of advice is never go to bed on an argument with your partner; you will only lie awake thinking about what has been said, and will find it almost impossible to get to sleep. Rose quartz may help here, as it soothes emotions.

Amethyst is very effective in producing a state of relaxation and a small tumblestone of amethyst under the pillow is said to help enormously with this problem. Other stones to consider are emerald, zircon, peridot and topaz. Diamond, with its ability to help clear the mind, may also be something to try, but could prove costly!

RESPIRATORY PROBLEMS

M any factors can cause difficulties with breathing. A cold or sinus problem can make it difficult to breathe properly, as can laryngitis, tonsilitis, bronchitis and hay fever. Any form of congestion on the lungs will also make things difficult, so do see your doctor if problems persist.

TREATMENT

Amber is said to be particularly effective in cases of bronchial disorders and asthma, pearl in clearing catarrh and helping with lung infections, pyrite in clearing sinus congestion and rutilated quartz in asthma and bronchitis. Turquoise may also be beneficial, as it helps with respiratory and circulatory problems.

Using gemstone elixir oils may be the best form of treatment but others may find sufficient help by merely holding their chosen stone.

Following a bout of 'flu or a heavy cold, or when feeling generally below par, using staurolite may help, as this stone often helps increase energy levels. Sometimes known as the 'fairy stone', these stones may be difficult to obtain in a pure form.

Persistent problems with breathing should always be referred to a doctor or physician for a full medical check-up.

HIGH BLOOD PRESSURE

B lood pressure readings tell us how hard the heart is working to pump the blood round the body; pressure can increase or decrease, depending on the level of activity being undertaken at the time.

TREATMENT

High blood pressure is very common among middle-aged people who lead sedentary lives or, conversely, jet-setting executives suffering stress! It can be a by-product of overeating, overdrinking, too much salt in the diet, being overweight, lack of exercise or a potential heart problem, such as the weakness of the heart or hardening of the arteries. High blood pressure can run in families but by watching the diet and exercising, its effects can be drastically lessened. Smoking should be reduced or, better still, given up altogether and the diet should show an increased consumption of fibre, a reduction in salt, sugar and fats, and a reduced intake of red meat and eggs.

Anything which will reduce stress should be considered. However, it would be quite wrong to suggest embarking on a stringent exercise regime if the person concerned has previously been inactive, as the disadvantages could outweigh any advantages. Changing lifestyle gradually is much more effective than a sudden change. Relaxation and cutting down on the amount of alcohol consumed could be sufficient to lower a high blood pressure reading.

The stones which may help are haematite and sodalite, both of which are good stress-reducers. Haematite is said to help reduce a rapid pulse rate while sodalite is often used by professional therapists to reduce high blood pressure. Taking up meditation should be considered and meditation with either of these stones could result in a considerable improvement in the condition.

TREATING STRESS

There are many other common health problems which can be

helped by the use of crystals and these have already been mentioned when each crystal and gemstone has been discussed. One of the most beneficial ways to use crystals and gemstones is often within the fields of mental and emotional well-being, and one of the biggest problems faced by us all at one time or another is stress.

One of the main problems in dealing with stress lies in identifying the cause of the problem. There may, indeed, be more than one cause and it is vital that these areas be targeted if the stress is to be successfully resolved. Some matters can be more easily dealt with than others: financial worries are unlikely, for example, to disappear overnight, whereas stress caused by other factors, such as overwork, can be reduced by reorganisation or reassessing the situation. A major cause of stress is the need to achieve; we often set ourselves unattainable goals and then feel stressed when we fail to achieve them. We need to give ourselves quality time alone to unwind. Gentle exercise is often a good way to reduce stress, and walking can be one of the most beneficial methods of stress-reduction.

When in a stressful situation, we need to create a balance, a calm, which will help to release any pent-up emotions. Learning to relax is the first stepping-stone to reducing stress levels. Meditation, especially with crystals and gemstones, may be the answer to creating this necessary balance. We have already discussed meditation with crystals in an earlier chapter and if you feel you are subjected to a lot of stress, try a simple meditation of 15 minutes or so, possibly using amethyst or rose quartz. You may also wish to consider the use of massage with gem elixir oils. Quietly allowing someone to carry out a gentle massage, with perhaps soft background music, can be very therapeutic in itself, and with the added help of the gemstones and crystals can indeed be a very relaxing experience.

Other crystals and gemstones known to be good to use for stress include agate, celestite, chrysoprase, garnet, rhodochrosite, tourmaline, alexandrite, dioptase, kunzite and onyx.

STRESS REDUCTION DURING SLEEP

Using crystals to help with sleep may also help reduce stress. A growing number of doctors now think that the greatest percentage of healing takes place while we are asleep because our mind is not active and our body is allowed to heal itself.

If you want to try using crystals in this way, programme your stone for the purpose, asking for healing, and either strap it to your wrist (most authorities suggest the left wrist) with gauze, or alternatively place a small tumblestone under your pillow. Contact with the crystal or gemstone in question is considered to be most beneficial. In addition, you may wish to try wearing your chosen stone, which should not be the actual stone used during the sleep process but another stone of the same kind. Again, this stone should be programmed for healing and you then can, when situations become exceptionally stressful, take time out on your own and give yourself a gentle massage in the temple area or sit and hold the stone and enter into a short meditation, asking for help and healing at the same time.

CARRYING A GEMSTONE

There is a variety of ways in which you can carry around your healing stone. Some people wear it as jewellery, others make a crystal pouch which can be sewn inside a garment and detached easily when the clothing needs washing. It should be remembered, however, that the stone will also need regular washing, cleansing, clearing and reprogramming, because it will be subject to the same dirt and pollution as the clothes you wear.

Should you decide to carry your gemstone or crystal around with you, make sure you touch it regularly, to reinforce the special bond. Think of it as a friend and companion and it will serve you well. Make sure that you let it see and feel sunlight. I make a point of talking to my stones, both those I carry around with me and those I have at home. If I have a problem, I tell my crystals, especially the

Bloodstone

Sardonyx
(red one side,
white the other)

Blue Lace Agate

*Labradorite
(shows flashes of blue
only when turned)*

Carnelian

Tectite

Emerald

Garnet

Sapphire

Ruby

Aquamarine

Topaz

Tourmaline

Citrine

Quartz Crystal

Moonstone

Turquoise

Tiger's Eye

Jet

Snowflake Obsidian

Amazonite

Amethyst Quartz

Calcite

Fluorite

Rose Quartz

Quartz chunk

Green Beryl

Pyrites

*Moss Agate
(a dense sample*

Coral

Red Jasper

Chalcedony

Petrified Wood

Pink and Grey Jasper

Green Agate

Lapis Lazuli

Agate Quartz

Agate with Fossils

Sodalite

Rutilated Quart

Amethyst Quart

one I carry around with me to help me in day-to-day situations; I ask the stone for help, telling it why and what I would ideally like from a situation.

Carrying around your own crystal or gemstone leads to a special bond. It also means that you always have a stone with you, should you have the time for meditation. Meditating can make personal troubles seem far less significant and thereby reduces stress.

Ꭰealing your pets

I know of many people who have tried using crystals to help their pets, with remarkable success. One lady attached a crystal inside the collar of her dog which suffered badly with mobility problems due to old age and arthritis. Having programmed the crystal in question specifically to help her pet, suffering jibes from her family and friends, she merely meditated regularly for healing to be given through the crystal she had used, regularly told the animal that he was receiving healing and would get well, and sat back and watched. Within a matter of a week or so, the dog showed a remarkable improvement. So much for the placebo effect! The dog most certainly didn't know that he was supposed to be feeling better but the improvement was considerable.

You may also wish to try the use of gem elixirs. In times gone by, it is recorded that farmers gave 'crystal water' (water that had been used to soak crystals in) to their sick farm animals, offering a prayer of healing for the animal at the same time. Perhaps this is something which should be re-instated. There is no reason why animals should not benefit from crystal and gemstone healing in the same way as mankind.

Conclusion

You should not be surprised if, on visiting a crystal therapist, use is made of stones other than those listed here for specific ailments. Many crystal therapists use stones with which they have experience, and in many cases, the choice of stones depends upon the therapist's own preferences and intuition. Crystal therapy uses both the energy of the healer and the energy of the crystal or gemstone and it is therefore important to have faith both in the stone and the person carrying out the treatment, should this not be yourself.

We will discuss visiting a crystal therapist in a later chapter, but let's first try a few questions.

PRACTICE

- Why is crystal and gemstone therapy more of a 'complementary' rather than an 'alternative' therapy?

- Which stone promotes relaxation and helps with insomnia?

- Why must you regularly clean stones you carry with you or wear?

- What is 'crystal water' and how was it used in the past?

LITHOMANCY

Having looked at the healing aspect of gemstones and crystals, we are now going to turn our thoughts to another use of the stones: lithomancy, casting the stones and using the patterns in which they fall to help us with our direction in life.

I doubt that there is anyone who has not, at some time or another, felt that they needed some help or guidance about what to do or which path to take in life. Using gemstones and crystals for this purpose is one of many types of help available among what are loosely termed 'New Age topics'. Others include tarot, runes, I Ching, numerology, palmistry and astrology. Many of these subjects are covered by books in the For Beginners *series.*

If you should decide to embark upon lithomancy for other people, I must stress the necessity to do so in a caring and considerate way. When people are troubled, they are looking not only for a sympathetic ear but also for help which should be clear, concise, yet thorough. However, it is not up to the person carrying out the reading to tell the other what to do. The art lies in making suggestions and offering choices and allowing the other person to make the choice they consider right for them. It is important that people maintain responsibility for their actions. It is also vital to be positive in what you are saying; do not end the reading on a negative note. You must be sincere, encouraging and helpful.

HOW TO START

Some professionals working in this field use only five stones, while others use several and others as many as 200. It is up to the individual to decide how many stones they wish to use and in which ways they want to use and interpret them.

The crystals you use for lithomancy must be specially programmed for this purpose and used for nothing else. Ideally, they should be kept separately from healing crystals and gemstones. You should also be aware of the need for regular cleansing, as many people may touch the stones; before they can be re-used, they need to be cleansed of any negativities they have picked up.

Most people keep their stones on a tray so they can be easily seen by the person seeking help and can be handled properly. You will also have to consider the surface onto which the stones are to be cast. Some people use sand trays, while others use silk cloths (black shows the stones off to their best advantage). Others, who have no strong feelings on this, merely cast the stones onto a table top.

Watch to see how the person chooses the stones. Some people will just pick up stones and others will take time choosing, looking at them over and over again before making a decision. You can learn from this what sort of individual you are dealing with and whether they are rash, intuitive or logical.

If you know something of the star sign of the person, it is interesting to see how this relates to their choice of stones. Virgoans, for example, are likely to choose colours that co-ordinate; Arians are likely to go for bright colours and have no changes of decision at all, unlike Librans who may spend a long time choosing their stones.

Meanings of the stones

We will now look at the meaning of 31 of the gemstones and crystals; it is up to you whether you decide to use all of these, some of these, or use a couple of the stones several times. You may, of course, decide to use others not listed here. The meanings given are traditional. Many professionals, however, may use slightly different meanings, based on intuition or psychic input, and you may be able to formulate your own meanings.

AGATE

A gates indicate increases of energy and surprises, and when seen in a reading suggest that the energy of the person concerned may be put to the test in an unexpected way.

AGATE QUARTZ

U sually representing a young man, many professional readers suggest this stone is the young man of the family, the son, or someone who is very close to the questionner.

AGATE WITH FOSSILS

F inances are represented by this stone, and there are possibilities of financial improvement, should opportunities be grasped. There is also a likelihood of a win on a lottery or a legacy of some kind, as there will definitely be an increase in money.

AMETHYST

A lovely, spiritual stone which shows an interest in personal development or philosophy. Most people who choose an amethyst will also choose the rose quartz, as they seem to interrelate, especially for healing. Someone who selects both of these stones is likely to be interested in, or capable of, spiritual healing. Amethyst can also indicate creativity, usually for the benefit of others.

AQUAMARINE

L ogic, rationality and clear thinking are represented by this stone, and anyone who chooses it may be sending out a message of lack of trust in what you are likely to be saying. They are in doubt about the validity of this form of self-help and may need extra persuasion that what is being said will really help them.

BERYL

Those people who pick the beryl are likely to be interested in spirituality, personal development, psychic powers and intuition. Should this stone appear in a reading, look to see if the amethyst and rose quartz are also present. If so, you have someone who may have a psychic talent which could be encouraged.

BLOODSTONE

Aches and pains, stresses and strains are usually associated with this stone when it appears in a reading. The problem could be in the past, present or future, and it is up to the reader to determine which this is. However, it does suggest that the questionner ought to slow down. Remember to phrase any advice of this nature in a helpful and positive way.

BLUE LACE AGATE

A young girl, probably within the family, is represented by this stone. As all agates are sensitive to other gemstones and crystals around them, it is necessary to look at the stones which surround the blue lace agate before making any firm statements. Should, for example, the bloodstone be next to the blue lace agate, with amethyst the other side, one could assume that there are possible health problems connected with a young girl with which the questionner may be able to help with healing.

CITRINE

A communication, usually a job offer, a new opening or a new relationship is represented by this lovely yellow stone. Again, it is necessary to look at the other stones in the area to see where this new beginning may lie.

CORAL

Someone who chooses the coral is likely to have undergone a transformation of some kind in the recent past and probably come through it better and wiser than before. This can relate to job, home, family or health and again, the reader must look to the other stones for help to decide in which area this transformation has taken place.

FLUORITE

Someone who picks this stone is likely to be artistic, creative and talented in some way, and to be able to earn money from the talent, should the wish be there to do so. The person drawing this stone may be over self-critical, fear failure and need to be convinced that their talent is worth pursuing.

GARNET

Garnets indicate good news, favourable communications, usually by post or telephone. Should the citrine be nearby, the news will probably be by telephone.

GREEN JASPER

Rejections in love are indicated by this stone should it be the dark green variety. The rejection can either be in a romantic relationship or in a family situation and feelings are likely to be strong. The person concerned may feel neglected and worthless or feel that the love they give is not returned in the same way. This may be an actual situation or how they perceive it. Should the green jasper be light rather than dark green, there will be happiness in love and general contentment.

JET

The drawing of this dark, black stone represents dark emotions, possible unfaithfulness and someone who is not willing to share. This could be the questionner or someone to whom they are close. Again, it is necessary to look at the surrounding stones before making a firm decision on who this stone represents.

LABRADORITE

Overseas travel, links with foreign shores, holidays perhaps, are all indicated by this stone. There may be travel for business or pleasure, communication from abroad, a relationship with a foreigner, or a summer holiday to the sunshine.

MOONSTONE

The person who chooses this stone may have difficulty distinguishing the real from the unreal, truth from reality, and be accused of daydreaming a lot of the time. Any artistic interests should be developed. The questionner should be advised to start something new which could be a challenge, rather than drift professionally.

MOSS AGATE

One of the best stones to see in a reading. The presence of this stone shows calm after a storm – a period of contentment after a period of anxiety and worry. Should this stone appear, you can assure the questionner that things are about to improve and all will be well. There will be much to look forward to in the future.

PETRIFIED WOOD

The appearance of petrified wood suggests legal papers, legal matters or the law in general. This could be something advantageous or not and again, the reader must look at the surrounding stones. There could be a will, a marriage, an agreement or contract, but conversely there could also be a divorce, trouble in a business matter, or a legal dispute of some kind.

PINK AND GREY JASPER

While green jasper indicates a young girl, pink and grey jasper indicate older people, either male or female. These could be parents or others close to the questionner who are considerably older. They will affect the questionner in some way, in hopes, plans and the future generally. There could be a legacy, an unexpected gift or older person who has to move in with the questionner due to health or other problems.

PYRITE

Iron pyrites, or 'fool's gold', were, to the inexperienced miner, often thought to be gold, hence the nickname, and the appearance of this stone in a reading indicates that all is not what it seems. There is deception or general mistrust around. Depending on the surrounding stones, the reader has to decide how to interpret this stone. It could suggest that someone needs to exercise caution in order not to be deceived. It can also mean that someone is very gullible and easily taken in. The person could be duped in a partnership or be contemplating embarking on a venture which needs careful consideration. When anyone chooses this stone, it should be suggested they think first and act later, rather than rush into something which may not be what it seems.

QUARTZ CRYSTAL

The return of good health, an increase in energy, vitality and stamina are all suggested by the presence of this crystal in a reading. If the questionner has been ill, it suggests the return of health and is a good sign. Should the questionner be a little unsure of a situation, this stone indicates a surge of energy which will take matters forward and a reliance on inner strength rather than other people. Success is suggested and achievements will be many.

RED JASPER

Jaspers calm troubled emotions and troubled minds and the presence of the red jasper in a reading suggests love, passion, jealousy and deep, strong emotions, especially if a large number are chosen. These emotions will relate to other people rather than situations.

ROSE QUARTZ

This healing stone indicates the questionner has healing capabilities, whether in personal 'hands on' healing, absent healing, or the ability to heal spiritually, especially if the aquamarine is close by.

RUBY

Those that choose the ruby are likely to be very fussy and demand perfection in everything and everybody. They often feel frustrated because they place unnecessarily high demands on themselves as well as on others and feel unable to meet their self-imposed standards. They fear failure. They may be obsessive and this is something which may be mentioned. They should be advised to be easier on themselves and on those close to them.

RUTILATED QUARTZ

The rutilated quartz is a lovely crystal. What appears to be a pale crystal has bright golden threads running through it and its appearance in a reading indicates artistic ability or creativity. The person who chooses this stone may already be earning a living from artistic pursuits or may be capable of doing so, perhaps without realising it and needing some persuasion to accept the talent, or may derive a great deal of pleasure from craft or handwork.

SAPPHIRE

Sapphires are stones indicating happiness, peace and harmony. If present in a reading, there is likely to be a period of happiness and contentment, although this may be short-lived.

SARDONYX

Weddings, engagements, proposals, love affairs, romance are all indicated by this stone. Most professionals suggest that the stone means a wedding, although not necessarily for the questionner. However, I personally feel that the stone refers to all love interests, and should not necessarily be taken to be a wedding.

TEKTITE

Tektite is a dull, black or brownish-looking stone, which is actually fused glass. It is not very appealing to the eye and is usually small. Probably formed by or from meteorites, its presence in a reading indicates a feeling of despair, depression, withdrawal or hopelessness. The person who chooses this stone may be suffering from these symptoms, although appearing to be cheerful. Alternatively, the presence of the stone may indicate someone in the questionner's surroundings who fits this picture. When this stone appears, see what other stones are also drawn. If the majority of them appear fairly optimistic, the depression may have passed.

TIGER'S-EYE

Self-confidence, independence but also loneliness are indicated by this stone's appearance. Someone who is very independent can also be very insular, as can someone who has been forced to stand up for themselves following a divorce or separation of some kind. This stone almost always indicates changes for the better, so should someone be going through a divorce, separation or loss of some kind, and feeling very alone and isolated, they should be made aware that the changes taking place will be for the best in the long run, for they will have learned and grown from the experience and will be wiser for it.

TOPAZ

The choosing of topaz suggests that there may be relationship difficulties and extreme care should be exercised, especially if the relationship is new. No firm statements should be made.

TURQUOISE

Anyone who draws the turquoise is likely to be a lucky person, seemingly protected from adversities. Peace, contentment and lasting happiness are assured. This is a very positive stone.

Layouts

Once the stones have been chosen, ask the questionner to cast them. You then decide which layout they most closely approach. If they do not seem to fall in a pattern, ask the questionner to throw them again, and perhaps again, until they do fall into a recognisable layout. We will discuss only four layouts here. Once you have gained experience with these four, you might want to draw up your own interpretations for other patterns.

Carrying out a reading will take time to do well and you should not expect to be able to achieve this until you have practised many times. Don't forget that the meanings of the stones need to be looked at in relation to the stones thrown next to them. You should also take into account the number of times the same stone has been chosen.

The zodiac layout

Based on 12 houses, the layout will look something like this:

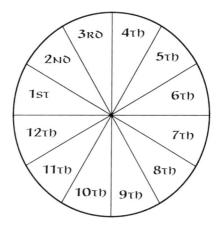

The meaning of the houses is as follows:

1st house   - the questionner
2nd house   - finances and material possessions
3rd house   - brothers, sisters, communication, short-distance travel
4th house   - home and family life
5th house   - children or lovers
6th house   - health, jobs or family pets
7th house   - partnerships, either personal or business
8th house   - sex, birth, life and death
9th house   - long-distance travel or study
10th house   - job or career, status and environment
11th house   - friends, hopes and wishes, group situations
12th house   - difficulties and fears

It is, of course, necessary to look at the stones chosen as a whole, and working from the 1st house through to the 12th, form a logical reading. Look at opposite houses when using this reading as well as adjacent houses. By exploring the meaning of each stone in each house and looking at stones in the opposite and adjacent houses, you will be able to build up a logical interpretation.

The Gypsy Layout

Draw a large circle on the floor. You may wish to have a circle made up of string readily available for this purpose. It should be at least 40 cm across. Thirteen stones should be chosen, plus a standard garden pebble. These should be taken in the left hand of the questionner and thrown into the circle. The pebble is said to indicate the questionner and is known as 'the significator'. Should this stone fall outside the circle and all others inside the circle, the stones need to be re-thrown. Tradition stipulates that should this happen for a second time, the whole exercise should be abandoned.

You should read the meanings of each of the stones, looking particularly at their distance from the significator and also at adjacent stones.

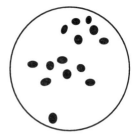

The random nine layout

The questionner takes any nine stones from the tray. Look to see how long they take in choosing, whether they seem to change their mind, whether they look at the stones in detail or not. All these things have a bearing on the reading you will give. Those people who just pick up any nine stones and throw them anywhere are likely to be rash, impulsive people who don't think things through. Those who spend time choosing them, arrange them in a nice pattern, colour co-ordinate them etc. are likely to be very organised, thorough, thoughtful and possibly apprehensive. Make a mental note of the stones which are picked up and then rejected – they may relate to events just passed or events with which the questionner feels uncomfortable.

Once the nine stones have been chosen, ask the questionner to lay them out however they like. Then ask yourself whether they lie all together in one group or in maybe two or more small groups. Are the groups all colour-related or related in another way, such as one group relating to people, another to personal circumstances etc.?

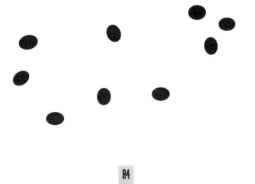

It is always prudent to ask the questionner whether there is one area of their life which requires more attention than the others. While it is good to give as much information as you can, the person will possibly only be waiting to hear about one aspect and will forget most of the rest of what is said.

Let's pretend we are doing a reading for a lady called Jo. She is 26, married with two small children (both boys) and she comes to you for advice on a potential business venture. She is worried that time away from home will upset her eldest son, who is very sensitive. She decides to draw nine stones and puts them in three groups:

GROUP 1   - agate quartz, green jasper, moss agate
GROUP 2   - petrified wood, pyrite, tiger's-eye
GROUP 3   - turquoise, rutilated quartz, quartz crystal

Group 1 refers to the situation regarding Jo's son (agate quartz). There is anxiety here, as shown by the green jasper, and yet the presence of the moss agate indicates that this period of anxiety is likely to be at an end. All will be well and she has been worrying about her son unnecessarily.

Group 2 refers to the setting up of a new company. Legal documents will be around (petrified wood), but she should watch what she signs (pyrite). She will need to be very independent (tiger's-eye) and she may have to make headway unaided.

Group 3 refers to the future. Turquoise is a positive stone, full of hope, calm and happiness. Rutilated quartz indicates that Jo's venture may revolve around her own artistic or creative nature, and although she may refuse to acknowledge that she is good at what she does, and seldom seems to get any support from others, she is likely to do well, as the turquoise is a very positive note in a reading. The quartz crystal suggests that she will have the inner strength to see her through, be full of energy and determination and will succeed, despite her fears.

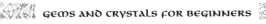
The 13 stone Layout

This layout, by tradition, uses stones other than gemstones or crystals. It was described to me by someone who uses pebbles from the beach. However, it seems so good that I see no reason why it couldn't be used with gemstones and crystals.

You need 13 stones. The first seven stones represent the planets of Mercury, Mars, Venus, Jupiter, Saturn, Sun and Moon. The other six represent situations, and are life and health, luck, magic, love, home and family and news.

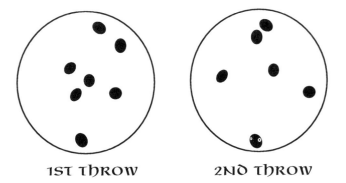

1ST THROW   2ND THROW

Each planet has a colour and it is best to use a stone which matches this colour. The seven colours are as follows, with some ideas on the types of stones to choose:

SUN	- yellow (citrine, rutilated quartz, dendritic agate)
MOON	- grey (moonstone)
MERCURY	- tan or sandy-coloured (rhodonite, amber)
VENUS	- green (green jasper, aquamarine)
MARS	- red (garnet, ruby, red jasper, carnelian)
JUPITER	- blue or blue-flecked (sodalite, turquoise)
SATURN	- black (jet, tektite, obsidian)

If possible, the stones should be about the same size. The other six stones should be coloured as follows:

Life	- blood-red (bloodstone)
Luck	- rose (rhodochrosite)
Magic	- pure white (quartz crystal)
Love	- rose-red or heart-shaped or both (rose quartz)
Home	- brown (petrified wood)
News	- multi-coloured (labradorite, amethystine agate)

Ask the questionner to take the planetary ones first, then concentrate on the question in hand and throw the stones into a circle, about 40 cm in diameter. The stones which land in the top right-hand portion of the circle are the ones of greater importance and represent the immediate future and influences. Look at the way the stones lie in relation to each other. Look at the ones in the top right-hand portion first and then the middle section. Generally most of the stones will lie near the middle of the circle and you should look to see if they form a pattern. Traditionally, triangles and circles are good shapes, whereas squares are not so good. Stones which touch each other increase the influences. Any odd stone which lies close to the bottom of the circle is of little significance.

A prominent Saturn stone indicates delays and limitations, while Jupiter represents career and finances. The Sun represents health, happiness and good fortune. Venus represents love, artistic matters, creativity and the feminine aspect, or the female in the life of a man. Mars represents energy, action, difficulties, troubles and the male aspect, or the male in the life of a female. Mercury is communication by letter, telephone, visit or journey. It can also represent doctors, nurses and the healing profession. The Moon represents change and possible delusions and double dealings, depending upon which are nearby.

Once you have looked at the planetary stones, remove them and ask the questionner to throw the other stones. If you are throwing onto sand, make sure you smoothe the sand over first.

The money and luck stones are the most important and should be dealt with first. Should, for example, the news and home stones fall together in the top right-hand portion, you could assume that there will be news coming relating to the home. If, on the other hand, the home and money stones fall together, you could interpret this as suggesting money is either coming into or out of the home. If the luck stone is also nearby, money might be coming into the home, possibly by means of a gift, windfall or legacy of some description.

Before we go on to look at the association between gemstones and the zodiac, take a few minutes to answer the practice questions here to consolidate your knowledge of what we have learned in this chapter.

PRACTICE

- What is 'lithomancy'?

- What can you learn about a person from watching how they choose the stones?

- What is the 'significator' and in which layout is it used?

- In the zodiac layout, what do the 3rd, 8th and 11th houses represent?

- Suggest three stones which might represent Venus and three which might represent news.

the zodiac

Gemstones have long been linked with the signs of the zodiac. Indeed, many students of astrology wear the gems associated with their sign, considering them to be lucky. Although it is not widely known, each sign has several possible associated gemstones. This is why stones are often referred to as 'having an affinity with' rather than being specific for a particular zodiac sign.

Those interested in astrology will know that the signs of the zodiac start with Aries and end with Pisces, so we are now going to go through each sign in turn and discuss the stones which are said to have an affinity with it. We will also discuss the planets associated with each sign, historical uses of the various stones and traditional folklores. As well as being associated with zodiac signs, stones may be related to months of the year and we will mention these associations.

ARIES, 21 MARCH–20 APRIL

Aries people are fiery types, ruled by Mars, so it should come as no surprise that the gemstone most usually associated with them is a red, fiery stone – the garnet. Also associated with Aries are the bloodstone, diamond, carbuncle and ruby.

GARNET

Garnets, most often associated with January birthdates, are a symbol of constancy and friendship and are said to warn the wearer when danger is near. Thought to be especially useful in cases of inflammatory diseases, they are useful for treating rheumatism, arthritis and inflammation of the joints. They are also used in dealing with blood problems, acting as a general tonic, aiding self-confidence and are also said to improve the sex drive! If worn on the left side of the body, garnets are believed to protect against depression as well as rheumatism and tradition suggests the wearing of garnets will bring business success and new opportunities.

BLOODSTONE

The bloodstone belongs to those Rams born during the month of March. Its flecks of red jasper fit in with the Mars and fire themes. Jasper is especially associated with stomach problems and is said to help with digestion if worn against the stomach area. Early Christians, who dedicated a gemstone to each apostle, dedicated jasper to St Peter. It is said that, to early Christians, bloodstone had an association with the blood shed by Christ at the Crucifixion. This is probably how it got its name. The story goes that on the hill of Calvary, some of the blood from the crucified Christ fell upon the green jasper that lay beneath the cross and speckled it with red.

Ancient civilisations thought it had the power to cause tempests and that it was a protection against drowning. The reasoning behind this is lost in antiquity. It was also used in seals, cameos and signets and many of the seals of the ancient Babylonians were cut in bloodstone.

DIAMOND

The diamond, one of the most precious stones, belongs in April. It is said to signify purity and innocence and it is for this reason that it is so often seen in engagement rings. Diamonds are supposed to be most powerful when combined with other gemstones and this could have led to the popularity of rings containing diamonds and other stones together. Very large diamonds are traditionally unlucky and there are many sad tales regarding the owners of unusually large diamonds.

Diamonds are crystalline forms of carbon and are the hardest stones known. It is said that diamonds belonged to Mars, the god of war (another link with Aries) and carrying one into battle protected the

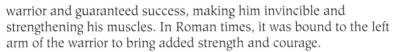

warrior and guaranteed success, making him invincible and strengthening his muscles. In Roman times, it was bound to the left arm of the warrior to bring added strength and courage.

The name 'diamond' comes from a word meaning 'indomitable', and the stone has always been associated with strength. Early Christians associated the stone with courage and it has always been thought to bring good luck. In the Middle Ages, it was said to help with madness, nightmares and in curing those who had been poisoned or subject to some form of pestilence.

It is only in recent centuries that diamonds have become such prized possessions, as in early days the ways in which they were cut led them to be dull and lacking in the sparkle with which they are now associated. The bloodstone and diamond worn together are said to be particularly lucky.

CARBUNCLE

The carbuncle and ruby are again fiery-red stones, fitting in with the Aries themes. In ancient times, it was felt that both carbuncle and ruby could protect against plague. The name 'carbuncle' comes from a word for coal and it is said to bring hope to unhappy situations. Carbuncles are believed to protect those travelling by land and sea and are very lucky if worn with the aquamarine.

RUBY

The ruby has always been associated with contentment and is considered to be a symbol of freedom and power, increasing energy levels. It is said to stimulate love if worn close to the heart. It is an aid in stimulating intuitive thought and is often used as a general tonic. It encourages selflessness and devotion.

This stone is especially valued in India, where it is found in river beds. Sinhalese legend calls rubies 'tears of Buddha' and it is a sacred gem to the Buddhists. It is one of the many stones which are said to stop bleeding and is also thought to help those suffering from sadness or melancholy. To the people of the Middle Ages, it was a token of friendship and it was believed that in times of trouble it would grow paler. There is a story that Catherine of Aragon wore a ruby in a ring on her little finger and as the love of her husband waned, so the stone became dull and pale. It is also recorded that the ruby set in the state crown of England had an unfortunate history – legend has it that Pedro of Castile so wanted the stone that he murdered the King of Granada to gain possession of it! Worn on the brow, the ruby is thought to give added insight and increased mental powers. Is also said to be able to ward off evil spirits, protect against poisons and act as an antedote to a snake bite.

TAURUS, 21 APRIL–21 MAY

The gemstone most usually associated with the Bull is the diamond, which we have already discussed. Those Bulls with April birthdates may find that the diamond is more suited to them than any other stone. However the other affinities, which more properly fit in with the characteristics of Taurus, are coral, emerald, lapis lazuli and jade. Sometimes you will also see sapphires being associated with Taurus, although I would dispute this connection. Taurus has as its planet Venus.

EMERALD

Emerald is a variety of beryl. Beryl has always been associated with the emotions. Emeralds symbolise serenity, success in love, wealth, happiness and peace of mind, and it's said they help with eyesight problems and restore youth (probably the two being linked). Thought to improve the memory and help in cases of insomnia, the emerald also strengthens the immune system. It is a good gemstone to use when meditating, as it assists in deeper spiritual insight. The emerald is considered the stone for May birthdays.

There is evidence that in Roman times wealthy people with eyesight problems wore emerald eye-glasses, and there are stories that the emperor Nero watched gladiatorial combat through an emerald to help his vision. Others considered that the emerald would help in healing ear problems. It has been said that emeralds will help cure ulcers, prevent fits and also ease childbirth! The Romans thought the emerald a remedy for the bite of poisonous spiders, whereas in the Middle East, it was said to ensure immortality. Other civilisations considered the emerald a deterrent against being possessed by demons and in India they were often used to decorate temples. In ancient times, due to the ease with which they could be cut, they were the most popular stone and were credited with many powers.

If you are in need of confidence, emerald is the stone to wear, as it encourages faith in your own abilities.

CORAL

Coral, which is not a true gemstone but a product of marine life, has always been associated with helping protect against malevolent attack ('the evil eye') and is usually pink, although sometimes white or red. The name comes from a Greek word for sea nymph. It has associations with stopping blood-flow, helping in cases of anaemia, giving wisdom and preventing madness. Plato suggested that it helped children with toothache and also kept sickness at bay, especially if worn around the neck. Red coral is said to relieve bowel disorders and skin problems and cleanse the system from impurities. Known to help with the throat and voice problems which beset Taureans, it is also said to strengthen the spleen and is another stone which is thought to lose its colour when the owner is ill.

JADE

Jade has always been popular with the Chinese. It appears in many of their temples and has been used in its powdered form as an internal treatment. In ancient times, jade was more highly prized than gold and was linked with eternity. The Maoris of New Zealand often use it in their weapons.

Traditionally associated with the month of May, it is said to relieve renal problems, protect wounds from becoming inflamed and to help with eye diseases. It is often linked with women, helping with all kinds of female disorders.

Yellow jade is thought to aid digestive problems. The stone is also said to assist wisdom and bring tranquillity, being credited with longevity and fertility. Jade is said to guard against lightning.

Lapis Lazuli

Lapis lazuli, or more properly 'lazurite', is a beautiful blue-green rock, whose name derives from the Arabic and Latin words for this colour. In ancient times referred to as the 'stone of Heaven', and more recently as the 'night stone', it is usually found in limestone near granitic rocks, enclosing grains of pyrite, especially in Italy, Chile and Turkey. It also has strong associations with the Egyptians, often being worn by them as a talisman to ward off danger. It too has been used to treat eye problems, powdered down to a paste, steeped in water and used as a poultice. It was also thought to be an aid in cases of epilepsy and a protection against hazards. More recently it has been used to help with thyroid problems and neuralgia.

It should be noted that lapis lazuli is a powerful gemstone and should therefore only be worn by those people who have sufficient strength of character and body to deal with its powers. Those of a sensitive nature may find it overpowering unless it is encased in glass or crystal. It is said to be particularly useful in treating thyroid problems and as an aid to enhancing psychic abilities, helping us to get in touch with our higher selves. It is a good stone to wear when decision making.

GEMINI, 22 MAY–21 JUNE

The stones associated with Gemini are agate (especially moss agate or banded agate, the latter showing lines of light and dark, red and white), beryl, chrysolite, onyx and peridot. The planet associated with Gemini is Mercury.

AGATE

Agates are types of chalcedony or cryptocrystalline quartz and are usually brown, dark red or yellow. Named after the river Achates in Sicily, they are now found in India, Brazil and Germany. For centuries they have been thought to bring luck to those people who work with or on the land.

The agate was held in great esteem by ancient civilisations who thought it was representative of the third eye and spiritual love. Probably the connection with the third eye also leads it to be used for eye problems and headaches. Ground to a powder, the stone was often used to stop bleeding and soothe irritations and skin diseases.

There are many types of agate but all agates are said to bring about good fortune, good health, eloquence, wealth and long life. Reputed to have been used by athletes since ancient times to increase vitality, the agate not only increases energy levels but also self-confidence, as it banishes fear. It was believed to help with epilepsy. The possession of an agate was traditionally thought to bestow the gifts of eloquence, social grace and good fortune on the owner. These earthy stones help to keep the Gemini grounded and promote truth. To strengthen its powers, the chrysoprase should also be worn.

BERYL

Beryl is usually green in colour, but sometimes has yellow, pink, blue and white shades within it. Known to have been one of the first crystals used by ancient seers, beryl is said to help those lacking motivation move forward by improving willpower.

In the Middle Ages, beryl was thought to cure laziness and banish fear and was linked with emotional difficulties. It was also said to help with asthma and kidney stones, as well as liver disease. In more recent times, the beryl has been used to treat throat problems and is a particularly good stone for meditation.

CHRYSOLITE

Chrysolite is most commonly an olive green colour but can also be brown or red. It gets its name from the Greek *chiastos* which means 'marked with an x'. For this reason, it is sometimes called 'the cross stone', and was also known as 'the golden stone' to the ancients.

It is said that to exert its full power, chrysolite should be set in gold. Known to be very useful in cases of viral illnesses, it is also used in cases of toxaemia. In ancient times, chrysolite was thought to be a cure for insomnia and protect against nightmares when worn at night, and when worn during the day, to dispel melancholy and improve creativity. In medieval times, it was believed to prevent madness.

ONYX

Onyx, a type of coloured chalcedony, has long been associated with improving concentration and devotion and it is not surprising, therefore, to see many rosaries made from this stone. It is also said to help with stress and aid inner serenity. It is used to improve concentration, self-control and hearing difficulties.

PERIDOT

Peridot is often recommended for sleeplessness, digestive problems, reducing stress and helping with lethargy by stimulating the mind. It is also said to help with lung congestion and stomach ulcers.

CANCER, 22 JUNE–23 JULY

Cancer's connections with the Moon are followed through in its gemstone associations, moonstone, chrysoprase, pearl and selenite. July's stone is traditionally ruby, which we have already discussed.

MOONSTONE

Moonstone is a variety of feldspar. It has a pearly appearance and can be grey, white, pale yellow or almost colourless. Said to grow stronger and weaker as the moon waxes and wanes, it is a symbol of hope and is especially protective to seafarers. The moonstone is so abundant in Ceylon that it is sometimes called the 'Ceylon opal'. In India, the moonstone was sacred for lovers.

It is said to help reduce fevers, promote long life and happiness and attract friendship. A feminine stone, used to help with menstruation and child-bearing, it maintains emotional balance and is sometimes called 'Mother Earth's stone'. It is used by men who wish to get in touch with the female side of their personalities and as an aid to understanding dreams.

In ancient times, this stone was said to protect travellers, especially those travelling by sea and was considered a protection against dropsy, fluid-retention and urinary problems.

chrysoprase

Chrysoprase is a bright green type of chalcedony and is sometimes called the 'joy stone', as it helps ease depression and anxiety, bringing joy, cheerfulness and personal insight. It should not be kept in direct sunlight, as this may cause the colour of the stone to fade. As it is said to improve memory and reduce nervousness, people often take it into exams with them. It also helps the mind to adapt to emergency situations.

In ancient times, it was believed that the stone would lose its colour if kept in the presence of poisons. Often worn as a remedy for gout and rheumatism, this stone was also used to treat kidney and bladder problems. Tradition suggests that it will strengthen the sight of anyone looking into it for any length of time.

This is said to be a particularly lucky stone if worn with agate.

selenite

Selenite or gypsum is reputed to be a rejuvenator, helping with many problems, ranging from improving skin texture to increasing fertility. Easily chipped and very soft, it is often used to relieve stress and help with nervous problems.

pearl

For centuries pearls have been considered an emblem of purity, innocence and peace. Pearls were great favourites in medieval times, and were thought to symbolise purity and chastity. Alchemists often dissolved pearls in lemon juice and gave the resultant liquid to patients suffering from internal bleeding, as well as many other types of internal problems. There are stories of their being ground to a fine powder and drunk in milk to cure irritability, weak eyes, consumption and the plague!

Associated with the month of June, pearls are particularly fortunate for those Cancerians with a June birthdate.

Pearls, being regarded as symbols of the moon, are often thought to be unlucky. Many people refuse to accept pearls as gifts, suggesting that they bring about an unhappy marriage. The reason behind this may lie with the fact that pearls can resemble tears and indeed, they have been described as 'solidified tears'. I personally do not believe any gemstone to be unlucky. If you care for your pearls and look after them, they can surely do you no harm.

Divers still wear pearls when in shark-infested waters, due to the tradition that they protect the wearer from such creatures.

Pearls are considered to be lucky when worn with emeralds and moonstones.

LEO, 24 JULY–23 AUGUST

The lion, ruled by the Sun, has as its stones amber, aventurine, topaz, onyx and diamond. Onyx and diamond have other affinities already discussed. July as a month has ruby as its association, whereas August has sardonyx, the stone of sociability.

SARDONYX

Sardonyx is a white and dark brown or red variety of onyx. Once believed to be a pain reliever, it is said to symbolise happiness in marriage and in friendship.

It was reputed to have the power to protect against the plague, stings and bites and give popularity to the wearer. It was widely used in Roman times and often found in brooches of the period due to the ease with which it can be engraved. Tradition suggested that unmarried women who wore the stone would never be wed but those who were married and about to give birth, were expected to find great comfort from this stone!

AMBER

Amber is formed from the fossilised and solidified resin of trees. It is often found in large lumps weighing many pounds and can be ground to make a powder to give for various internal complaints or burnt to provide an aromatic vapour. It is said to help with heart problems and to help ward off the plague and curses by absorbing negativities. It is a harmonising stone, which can be of great help in the relief of stress, asthma and as a de-toxifier. It is sometimes called the 'mindful stone' because it is said to contain within it vibrations from the past and increase memory.

In ancient times, amber was often worn around the throat as a protection against catarrh, asthma and hay fever, and when powdered and mixed with oil was used as a body preparation to ease aching muscles. Thought to help with bronchial problems, it was used for the mouthpieces of tobacco pipes in times gone by.

Other stones which are closely related to amber include krantzite and beckerite.

AVENTURINE

There are two different minerals called 'aventurine' – the one I refer to here is the green quartz rather than the feldspar also known as 'sunstone'. Aventurine is said to purify and strengthen the body, mind and spirit. Those suffering from anxiety might find it offers some relief by helping them to focus on their problems. A stone associated with bringing good health and well-being, this gemstone is another reputed to help with exam situations. Those who suffer from migraines may also find the stone useful, as discussed earlier.

TOPAZ

Topaz, also associated with November and with Jupiter, is a stone with a wide tradition of applications – ranging from childbirth to warding off the plague. It is found in pink, yellow, green, blue or white forms.

Topaz can be changed by heat, pressure and friction, and is a stone exhibiting strong electric currents. Said to be able to detoxify the body and regenerate organs and glands, the stone helps to soothe and give inner peace to those with problems. Affected by the phases of the moon, it reputedly helps with eye disorders, cures baldness, prevents asthma and helps with sleep disorders when used as a gem elixir. Said to promise its owner a long and happy life, it is associated with faithfulness. Eastern mystics believe it helps ease the pain of death and enables those who use it during meditation to see into the future.

Tradition suggests that if it is worn on the left-hand side of the body it can help overcome grief and if worn over the stomach it will protect the wearer from stomach disorders by calming negative emotions. Since ancient times it has been used to help with female disorders, lung complaints, epilepsy, bladder troubles and problems with the nose and throat. The amethystine sapphire will increase the power of the topaz.

VIRGO, 24 AUGUST–23 SEPTEMBER

Agate, jasper, tourmaline, chalcedony and carnelian are all associated with Virgo, whereas September has associations with the sapphire. Virgo is another sign ruled by Mercury.

SAPPHIRE

Sapphires have for centuries been regarded as highly spiritual stones. It is said that a ring containing diamonds and sapphires will be exceptionally lucky, sapphires always having been associated with luck in romance. Said to bring peace and happiness, this stone will help with the heart and stomach and also with stimulating the pituitary glands and psychic centres. Its primary role, however, lies in the field of mental health.

In ancient times it was used to treat eye disorders and as an amulet to give protection from bewitchment and to guard the chastity of its owner, dimming if there were signs of fraud or treachery.

The power of the sapphire will be increased if it is worn with the turquoise stone.

TOURMALINE

Tourmaline generally ranges from dark green to black, although other colours are fairly common. It is a healing stone, which will enhance the healing potential of other stones with which it is kept in contact. Used by astrologers in the past at times of planetary change to ease the transitions (it wards off negative energy), it should be worn next to the skin for best effect. It is said to help with nervous troubles, stress-related problems and give confidence and protection by reducing negativities, and so is another stone which is often taken into exam rooms.

Often carried in ancient times as an amulet, it is believed to give added perception to its wearer.

chalcedony

Chalcedony, named after the Greek city of *Chalcedon*, is a bluish-grey stone seldom used but said to be useful in cases of bad temper or unease, bringing about feelings of peace and serenity. As such, it is a gemstone which should have many applications in our modern world!

Believed by the ancients to give physical strength and heal gallstones, it was also used to deliver people from nightmares.

carnelian

Carnelian is usually red in colour but can also be brown and off-white. It is sometimes called the 'blood stone' and was used in times gone by to stop the flow of blood, especially nosebleeds. Carnelian is a strong gemstone reputed to be a powerful healer, helping to balance and energise the body, and particularly useful in gallbladder and liver problems.

Popular in Arab countries and found in inlays on jewellery and sarcophagi, the stone is thought to promote long life and eliminate fear by keeping the wearer 'grounded' and rational. Helpful with nervous problems when worn next to the skin, good fortune is said to follow those who carry the stone.

In more modern times it has been used to increase creativity in speech and mind and many public speakers carry carnelian with them.

LIBRA, 24 SEPTEMBER–23 OCTOBER

Strongly associated with the opal (considered by many to be unlucky), rose quartz, emerald and malachite are also stones with an affinity for the Libran. Venus is the planet for Librans.

OPAL

The opal was once considered a symbol of hope, bringing the wearer love and lasting happiness. It is a stone defying description, as it contains fire sparks, delicate colours and a full spectrum of colour. Formed from the skeletons of tiny shells and animals, opals are very porous and are at least thirty per cent water. As a consequence of this, they should never be immersed in water or brought into contact with oils – those with opal rings take note!

To the ancients, especially the Greeks and Romans, the opal was thought to give direction if held between the eyes and was known as the 'stone of vision' or 'gem of hope'. They also believed it would look after both children and the arts and was described as 'the gem of the Gods'.

A strong healing stone, said to enhance intuition, help with eyesight (it is sometimes called the 'ophthalmois' or 'eye stone') and bring relaxation, to the point of total peace, this stone can be used to put the wearer in touch with his or her higher self. It is reputed to lose its lustre if touched by an unfaithful lover, and was considered to be unlucky because of its variable colour. Used by those with lung complaints, it is also said to help with the assimilation of proteins into the system.

The opal will increase in power if worn with the lapis lazuli and is especially helpful to those born in October.

MALACHITE

Malachite is another healing stone, its green stripes having the ability to soothe and bring about restful sleep, as well as aid in circulation difficulties and balance the emotions. Containing copper, this stone is also useful in treating cases of rheumatism (those affected by this complaint may like to know that other copper-based stones are turquoise and chrysocolla) and toothache. It is also called the 'peacock stone', a name given to it in Roman times, when it was believed to help with colds, bleeding, vertigo and teething problems in babies. It is said to attract love to its wearer and in the USA is thought to bring wealth (or love of money!). Malachite is an exceptionally good stone to use in meditation.

ROSE QUARTZ

Rose quartz is said to be capable of changing negative energies into positive energies. It is often called the 'stone of unconditional love', pink being associated with this quality. It is thought to help diffuse stressful situations and heal emotional wounds when kept in a living room.

Excellent to use for migraines and headaches, rose quartz promotes peace and healing, stimulates the imagination and intellect and reduces feelings of anger, resentment and guilt. Said to increase fertility (possibly because of its association with love), the stone is one of the strongest healing stones available.

SCORPIO, 24 OCTOBER–22 NOVEMBER

Magnetite, obsidian, smoky quartz, jasper and aquamarine are all associated with the Scorpion, whilst November is associated with topaz. Mars and Pluto are the associated planets.

AQUAMARINE

Aquamarine is usually a blue-green colour, but can also be yellow and is another 'exam stone'. Said to banish nerves and fear and protect the wearer from poisons, it is most often used for ridding a person of unhappiness. This is a stone of happiness in marriage and well-being, bringing clarity of mind and purpose to its wearer. Aquamarine is also reputed to help with glandular problems, disorders of the throat, stomach and eyes and fluid-retention. Often used in meditation, this stone from the beryl family is thought to protect the wearer from accidents, especially when travelling by sea.

To increase the power of this stone, it should be worn with the carbuncle.

OBSIDIAN

Obsidian is volcanic lava and is often used to improve poor eyesight. Considered to be a 'male' stone, probably because when cut and polished it makes effective spearheads and knife blades, it is said to help those embarking upon a spiritual quest, keeping energies stable and clearing blockages. It is said that those who wear this stone will never shed tears of grief. Reputed to be a powerful healer, this is another stone which needs to be used wisely and only by those capable of dealing with its power.

SMOKY QUARTZ

Smoky quartz has for generations been considered a good luck charm or talisman, often being given to soldiers about to go into battle. An aid in relieving negativity and promoting relaxation, this is another stone often used in meditation, and if kept under a pillow at night, it is said to induce lucid dreams. The ancients considered the smoky quartz helpful in cases of infertility.

A word of warning concerning smoky quartz – genuine smoky quartz is produced by natural radioactive materials. However, it can also be man-made, in which case it is usually very dark or black. True smoky quartz should be brown. It is always preferable to use the natural stone, as man-made stones do not have the same qualities and the healing properties will be impaired.

MAGNETITE

Magnetite is not often used, but is particularly useful in cases of rheumatism. Said to be an energy restorer, this black stone is sometimes also called 'lodestone' and is useful for meditation, as an aid in acquiring wisdom and intuition. It may also be able to help in cases of liver problems and even in premature baldness.

SAGITTARIUS, 23 NOV–21 DEC

Amethyst, spinel, sapphire and turquoise are all associated with Sagittarius, whereas topaz is often connected with the month of November. Jupiter is connected with Sagittarians.

amethyst

Amethyst, together with rose quartz, is probably now one of the most popular gemstones. Ancients thought it was a cure for drunkenness, probably because its name comes from a Greek word implying sobriety, and those who wore it believed that they could drink as much as they wished without suffering any ill-effects. The Romans, often used amethyst cups to help the drinker to remain sober. However, because of the darkness of the cups, the contents could be well-watered without anyone noticing and perhaps this is why they stayed sober! It is reputed to lose its brightness in the presence of poison and to pale if the wearer is ill.

Also associated with the month of February, the amethyst gives serenity and steadfastness and has long been associated with St Valentine, bringing happiness in love and good luck. Often used in religious circles both in rings and rosaries, an amethyst wrapped in thin silk and held over the temples is said to soothe nervous headaches. Tradition suggests that the stone should, however, first be warmed either by the sun's rays or the warmth of a natural fire.

Considered to be a spiritual stone, the amethyst has long had the reputation of being able to increase the owner's ability to develop spiritually, purify and heal, and is very commonly used by healers to induce calm and alleviate stress and loneliness. Used in meditation, for guidance and help, the amethyst will help bring clear thoughts and calm the mind as well as help with headaches. I have used it for this purpose and can vouch for these claims. A very powerful stone, the amethyst provides a link between the higher and lower states of consciousness.

During the Middle Ages the amethyst was quite rare and was highly prized and it is still used in the rings of Roman Catholic bishops. It has been connected with Sagittarius since the beginnings of modern astrology.

spinel

Spinel, sometimes also called 'spinal ruby', is usually a lovely red colour. It is said to give added strength of purpose to its owner and bring clarity of mind, especially in business matters. Thought by the ancients to prevent damage from storms, it is now said to help in cases of nausea and sickness.

TURQUOISE

Turquoise, associated with December birthdays and so most properly used by those Archers born then, was used as a charm by Indian medicine men, who valued it as a powerful healer. Some American Indians still consider the stone to be sacred.

Reputed to be a love charm and another stone believed to change colour if the lover is unfaithful or, indeed, if its wearer is close to death, it is also considered to be a stone of friendship and loyalty. Should your turquoise start to pale, don't worry – simply leave it off for a few weeks and it should return to its normal brilliance.

Used in ancient times to ward off accidents and given as a comfort to those about to undergo surgery. Those people who travel on horseback may wish to wear this stone, as it is said to ensure the horse's surefootedness.

Thought to bring prosperity and luck, especially if worn with a sapphire, the turquoise is reputed to promote the regeneration of cells, protect against pollutants and strengthen the body. It is believed to help with bad eyesight and if applied to the chest area in a poultice, to help with bronchial problems.

Traditionally, the turquoise stone should be a gift and it is considered to be unlucky to buy your own. It is particularly powerful if worn with the blue sapphire.

CAPRICORN, 22 DECEMBER–20 JANUARY

Jet and tiger's-eye are associated with the Goat, and January, as already mentioned, is associated with the garnet. Capricorn is ruled by Saturn.

JET

Considered to be a magical stone by the ancient Britains, jet is a fossilised plant and not a stone at all. In early British history, it was frequently used to repel curses and the plague, when burnt. It was taken powdered in wine and water as a cure for toothache or when teeth became loose. Also used to help in skin problems, prevent hysteria and help with many female disorders, it was said to counteract magic spells and protect the wearer from bites. Popular with Queen Victoria who wore it after the death of Prince Albert, it became synonymous in the latter part of the nineteenth century with women in mourning. It was also used in amulets to prevent hallucinations.

In more recent times, the jet has been used to treat migraine and is another substance which can be faked – plastic, rubber and glass have all recently passed as jet.

Jet is particularly powerful if worn with the ruby.

TIGER'S-EYE

Tiger's-eye, another quartz, is a very useful stone for many Capricorns and also for those people who worry about their health, as it is said to guard against hypochondria and psychosomatic illness. Giving a feeling of confidence and inner strength, it is said to encourage creative pursuits, calm and balance.

Traditionally used for healing problems with the lower legs and feet, it was also considered useful for healing eye problems, probably due to the name of the stone rather than any special qualities. Known to be useful in digestive problems (especially those of a nervous origin), it can be particularly useful to Capricorns who are stubborn and intransigent, as it is said to 'ground' and balance.

AQUARIUS, 21 JANUARY–19 FEBRUARY

Amethyst, chalcedony, aquamarine and turquoise are all associated with Aquarians and as these stones are also associated with other signs they have already been discussed. Aquarius is also connected with lepidolite, zircon and celestite. Aquarians are ruled by Saturn and Uranus.

LEPIDOLITE

A very unusual stone, lepidolite has a high lithium content and is very helpful in balancing out the compulsive behaviour for which Aquarians are notorious. Also useful as an aid to psychic development, the lepidolite will help to inspire, illuminate and develop the link between the conscious lower mind and the higher mind.

Used with kunzite, another unusual stone, the results are said to be quite spectacular, especially in developing healing talents.

CELESTITE

Celestite is a relaxing stone, helping its owner to unwind from even the most stressful circumstances, and aiding and accelerating spiritual growth and creative expression. Said to impart clear speech and clarity of thought, this stone should, in truth, be far more popular in this modern age.

ZIRCON

Zircon is a multi-coloured stone helping to calm emotions and protect against depression. Its ability to help raise self-esteem and gain spiritual insight make it another true New Age stone. Used by the ancients to help treat fevers, the zircon is also useful in cases of insomnia and is said to increase the appetite.

PISCES, 20 FEBRUARY–20 MARCH

Crystal, chrysolite and bloodstone are connected with Pisces. The ruling planet for Pisces is Neptune.

CRYSTAL

Crystal, quartz crystal or rock crystal, is probably the most powerful stone known to mankind. Used in modern technology and by many as an aid to meditation, crystal releases the owner's higher consciousness and can accelerate spiritual growth, spiritual development, and healing.

Tradition suggests that a cup made of quartz crystal will turn cloudy if poison is added to the liquid to be drunk and so in ancient times many goblets were made of crystal. The ancients used it to amplify the rays of the sun and bring heat to the body, as well as in a powdered form for many types of ailment.

Probably the most powerful general healer, the quartz crystal attracts energy and light and is often employed as an aid in psychic development, facilitating meditation, dispelling negativity and inspiring communication with the higher self. Quartz crystal is often used as a charging crystal for other stones and is widely used in the East for magical purposes in the form of charms and talismans. It is said to promote a deep sleep if worn at night and protect against evil.

It is particularly powerful if worn or used with amethyst.

We have now covered all the signs of the zodiac and the stones associated with them. Whatever your birth sign, ruling planet or best-aspected planets, I truly feel that you can be attracted to a particular stone. Should this happen to you and the stone does not appear in the list of stones for your sign, please don't turn away from the stone you had chosen. There may be several reasons why you are drawn to purchase a stone at a particular time and as a result, the right stone for you may have no connection whatsoever with your birth sign or planets. Remember, you are an individual; trust your own instincts and always be true to yourself.

There is a wealth of information in this chapter and I do not expect you to be able to remember all the details, so we'll finish with some questions of a general nature.

PRACTICE

- Which stone did the Romans believe helped with eyesight and how did they use it?

- Why was the emerald so popular in ancient times?

- Which stone was thought to represent the 'third eye'?

- Why are pearls considered to be unlucky?

- What is amber?

CONCLUSION

Modern technology seems to drive us further and further away from natural remedies, actions and thoughts. Crystals and gemstones have been with us a very long time – in fact they predate the evolution of human beings. They are part of this planet in the same way as we are, and form part of the order of the universe.

Gemstones and crystals, if used properly, wisely and well, can help in many forms of healing, meditation, self-development, self-awareness and personal growth. As we have seen, there are many and varied crystals to choose from and only practice will ensure their correct use.

Much modern thought on crystals and gemstones is confusing. Please don't expect to be a professional crystal therapist having read this one book. This takes years of study and practice, and even then, as most therapists will tell you, you continue to learn.

In the appendices that follow, we shall briefly discuss visiting a crystal therapist, take a look at pyramid power, and, finally, have a bit of fun with 'lucky stones'.

APPENDIX 1
VISITING A CRYSTAL
THERAPIST

You should try to ensure that the person you are visiting is indeed a professional crystal therapist. Such people should have a diploma or qualification from an organisation such as the British Society of Dowsers or the Institute of Crystal and Gem Therapists and be aware of the law pertaining to treatment. If you visit a therapist and there is no sign of a certificate, you are within your rights to ask to see one before commencing any treatment. If you have any doubts, check their qualification out with the organisation concerned before starting therapy.

There is always a large degree of trust involved in healing, not least in crystal therapy, and that trust can easily be betrayed by unscrupulous people out to make easy money. Beware of any therapists who recommend visits more than twice a month, unless the problem is severe or involves auric healing, and of people charging exceptionally high fees for their services. Most therapists have a set scale of charges. You should check costs before attending for an appointment, to avoid embarrassment both to yourself and the practitioner concerned. There should also be a set length of time for consultations, which will be strictly adhered to. At the beginning of your treatment, your chosen therapist should be able to give you an estimate of the final cost.

It is also worth noting that no therapist of repute will treat a person under the age of 16 without written, parental permission. The parent should, if possible, accompany the child for the course of treatment.

In addition to the types of healing already mentioned in this book, crystal therapists may also use other forms of treatment. While it is not recommended that beginners try any of these. I will discuss these briefly here so that a potential patient is aware of what might happen.

Zone therapy   Used for healing of hands and feet, this therapy uses the crystal as a massage tool. Usually a small, thin, single-terminated quartz will be used to stimulate acupuncture points and lymphatic systems.

Neural zone therapy   Used mainly for chronic imbalances, epilepsy, arthritis and nervous problems, a large crystal and control crystal are used in conjunction with 'stickers' attached to the relevant part of the body.

Allergy testing   Using a pendulum in most cases, the therapist will ask for certain responses and may also use a list of vitamin or mineral deficiencies to test for the allergy, as well as a list of three or more reasons for the allergy. These could include physical contact, internal digestion or outside/environmental substances.

There are obviously other types of treatment that you could meet when visiting a crystal therapist but the main requisites are that you have faith in the therapist, faith in the crystals and gemstones used and feel free to ask questions.

APPENDIX 2
PYRAMID POWER

Many crystal therapists use pyramids when carrying out healing, suggesting that they enhance the healing powers and provide a stable energy field. The pyramid must always face magnetic north and not be edge-ways on. The most energised place on a pyramid's surface is said to be one third of the way up.

You can place pyramids on the chakras for healing and coloured pyramids can be used to correspond to the colour of the individual chakra. This will provide very thorough healing. Should you wish to use pyramids and crystals together, use your intuition to choose the crystals or gemstones for the pyramid/chakra healing.

You can easily make your own pyramid, preferably out of a pure material, and it is said that copper strips attached to each edge of the pyramid will enhance its energies. If you do make your pyramid out of metal make sure you cut triangles into all four sides. This is a traditional requirement. You can also buy pyramids made from crystal and other gemstones. I have one made of onyx.

To energise a pyramid and its contents (crystals and gemstones), place quartz crystals on the four corners of the pyramid. Amethyst and moonstone are said to be good crystals for night-time energising under a hollow pyramid. You can also use your pyramid for purifying crystals and gemstones. Said to be especially useful before healing, pyramids are thought to speed up the preparation of gem elixirs.

APPENDIX 3
LUCKY AND
UNLUCKY STONES

Many stones are considered to be lucky and since early times, beads have been used as means of protection. Some of these we have already discussed but there are many others. Beads made of onyx are supposed to be exceptionally lucky, as they avert danger and bring success in love affairs. Amber beads worn at a wedding are thought to bring luck, the husband proving faithful and the union being blessed by many children. In Italy amber necklaces are worn to help with laryngitis, while in Russia they are worn to bring long life and happiness. Coral beads, by tradition, are also used to promote good health, while jet will help to inspire courage and hope. Buddhists prize the diamond, sapphire, coral, ruby and cat's-eye, while the Hindus use a sacred necklace made of crystal or shell.

For those people interested in astrology, having considered the stones mentioned for their signs, it is worth pointing out that some sources believe that some stones are to be avoided at all costs. These are as follows:

ARIES	- avoid ruby, jet and pearl
TAURUS	- avoid garnet, chrysolite, sardonyx and jacinth
GEMINI	- avoid carnelian and jade
CANCER	- avoid opal and lapis lazuli
LEO	- avoid aquamarine and carbuncle
VIRGO	- avoid agate, topaz and chrysoprase
LIBRA	- avoid ruby, jet and pearl
SCORPIO	- avoid garnet, chrysolite, sardonyx and jacinth
SAGITTARIUS	- avoid jade
CAPRICORN	- avoid opal and lapis lazuli
AQUARIUS	- avoid aquamarine and carbuncle
PISCES	- avoid agate and topaz

In addition to these, the following should be borne in mind:

amethystine sapphire	- exceptionally lucky to Sagittarians
haematite	- exceptionally lucky to Arians
white sapphire	- exceptionally lucky to Pisceans
serpentine	- exceptionally lucky to Capricornians
magnetite	- exceptionally lucky to Scorpios
jargoon	- exceptionally lucky to Aquarians
jacinth	

For those people whose lucky stone is emerald, the moonstone will enhance the luck, provided it is not on the 'unlucky list' for your particular star sign.

Other traditional suggestions include linking lucky stones with hours of the day and days of the week. For those who are interested, and have sufficient money to be able to purchase all of these stones, the list is given in a table on pages 116–117.

We have now looked at most of the main features of gemstones and crystals – their colour, healing potential, zodiac relations and their links with other esoteric forms and therapies.

I hope reading this book has stimulated a real and lasting appreciation of the value of gemstones and crystals and you will want to find out more about them. There are many books available on the subject and some of these are listed on page 118. Let the beauty and strength of the stones into your life and use them wisely and well.

HOUR	SUNDAY	MONDAY	TUESDAY	WEDNESDAY	THURSDAY	FRIDAY	SATURDAY
1 AM	Diamond	M'stone	H'matite	Jasper	C'buncle	Coral	T'quoise
2 AM	Coral	T'quoise	Diamond	M'stone	H'matite	Jasper	C'buncle
3 AM	Jasper	C'buncle	Coral	T'quoise	Diamond	M'stone	H'matite
4 AM	M'stone	H'matite	Jasper	C'buncle	Coral	T'quoise	Diamond
5 AM	T'quoise	Diamond	M'stone	H'matite	Jasper	C'buncle	Coral
6 AM	C'buncle	Coral	T'quoise	Diamond	M'stone	H'matite	Jasper
7 AM	H'matite	Jasper	C'buncle	Coral	T'quoise	Diamond	M'stone
8 AM	Diamond	M'stone	H'matite	Jasper	C'buncle	Coral	T'quoise
9 AM	Coral	T'quoise	Diamond	M'stone	H'matite	Jasper	C'buncle
10 AM	Jasper	C'buncle	Coral	T'quoise	Diamond	M'stone	H'matite
11 AM	M'stone	H'matite	Jasper	C'buncle	Coral	T'quoise	Diamond
NOON	T'quoise	Diamond	M'stone	H'matite	Jasper	C'buncle	Coral

hour	SUNDAY	MONDAY	TUESDAY	WEDNESDAY	THURSDAY	FRIDAY	SATURDAY
1 PM	C'buncle	Coral	T'quoise	Diamond	M'stone	H'matite	Jasper
2 PM	H'matite	Jasper	C'buncle	Coral	T'quoise	Diamond	M'stone
3 PM	Diamond	M'stone	H'matite	Jasper	C'buncle	Coral	T'quoise
4 PM	Coral	T'quoise	Diamond	M'stone	H'matite	Jasper	C'buncle
5 PM	Jasper	C'buncle	Coral	T'quoise	Diamond	M'stone	H'matite
6 PM	M'stone	H'matite	Jasper	C'buncle	Coral	T'quoise	Diamond
7 PM	T'quoise	Diamond	M'stone	H'matite	Jasper	C'buncle	Coral
8 PM	C'buncle	Coral	T'quoise	Diamond	M'stone	H'matite	Jasper
9 PM	H'matite	Jasper	C'buncle	Coral	T'quoise	Diamond	M'stone
10 PM	Diamond	M'stone	H'matite	Jasper	C'buncle	Coral	T'quoise
11 PM	Coral	T'quoise	Diamond	M'stone	H'matite	Jasper	C'buncle
12 PM	Jasper	C'buncle	Coral	T'quoise	Diamond	M'stone	H'matite

FURT)ER READING

Baer, Randall and Vicki, *Windows of Light*, Harper and Row, 1986
Bonewitz, Ra, *Cosmic Crystals: Crystal Consciousness and the New Age*, Aquarian Press, Northants., 1983
Caldecott, Moyra, *Crystal Legends*, Aquarian Press, Northants., 1992
Cayce, Edgar, *Gems and Stones*, A.R.E. Press, Virginia Beach, USA, 1979
Flammonde, Paris, *The Mystic Healers*, Stein and Day, New York, 1974
Galde, Phyllis, *Crystal Healing: The Next Step*, Llewellyn, USA, 1991
Gurudas, *Gem Elixirs and Vibrational Healing*, Cassandra Press, USA, 1985
Harold, Edmund, *Crystal Healing*, Aquarian Press, Northants., 1987
Hodges, Doris M., *Healing Stones*, Pyramid Press, USA, 1961
Irwin, Neil, *Understanding Crystals,*, Aquarian Press, Northants., 1991
Markham, Ursula, *Fortune Telling by Crystals and Semiprecious Stones*, Aquarian Press, Northants., 1987
Stein, Diane, *The Woman's Book of Healing*, Llewellyn, USA, 1987
Uyldert, Mellie, *The Magic of Precious Stones*, Aquarian Press, Northants., 1981